Wood Furniture Projects

F. RICHARD BOLLER

State University of New York—Buffalo

Wood Furniture Projects

Bobbs-Merrill Educational Publishing
Indianapolis

Educational Consultant
Rex Miller, Ed. D.
State University of New York—Buffalo

The Bobbs-Merrill Company, Inc.
4300 West 62nd Street
Indianapolis, Indiana 46268

First Edition
First Printing 1979
Designed by Sandra Strother-Young

Library of Congress Cataloging in Publication Data

Boller, Richard
  Wood furniture projects.

  SUMMARY: A textbook for individuals with wood shop experience, designed to help them select and plan a variety of wood furniture projects.
  1. Furniture making—Amateurs' manuals. [1. Furniture making. 2. Woodwork] I. Title.
TT195.B64   684.1'042   78-26609
ISBN 0-672-97269-7

Contents

Preface ix
Acknowledgements xi
Shop Safety Rules and Practices xiii

SECTION I: DRAWING TABLES

Unit 1. Free-form Drawing Table   **2**
Enlarging a pattern, use of fixtures, *shaping a free form,* through mortise, keyed tenon

Unit 2: Conventional Drawing Table   **7**
Doweled base, drawer construction, drawer side guides, *bolted assembly*

SECTION II: THREE-DRAWER CHESTS

Unit 3: Three-Drawer Dresser   **12**
Veneered plywood, skeleton frames, solid wood trim, routing and shaping, drawer construction, metal drawer runners, *sculptured feet*

Unit 4: Three-Drawer Chest   **16**
Veneered plywood, *skeleton frames,* solid wood trim, routing, drawer construction, *center drawer guides,* solid base

Unit 5: Three-Drawer Dresser   **20**
Veneering, panel and frame construction, skeleton frames, solid wood trim, *drawer construction,* drawer center guides

SECTION III: HOPE CHESTS

Unit 6: Utility Hope Chest   **26**
Veneered plywood, rabbet and groove joints, solid wood trim, routing, cedar lining

Unit 7: Early American Hope Chest   **29**
Veneered plywood, *splined miter* and groove joints, solid wood trim, routing, *scalloped base,* decorative drawer fronts, *wagon seat top trim*

SECTION IV: ONE-DRAWER NIGHTSTANDS

Unit 8: Early American Nightstand   **34**
Veneered plywood, skeleton frames, rabbet and dado joints, *solid wood trim, routing, scalloped base,* drawer construction

Contents

Unit 9: Provincial Nightstand   **38**
Veneered plywood, skeleton frames, rabbet and
dado joints, *solid wood trim, routing,* solid base,
drawer construction, *formica top*

SECTION V: UTILITY CABINETS

Unit 10: Entertainment Center   **44**
Veneered plywood, *edge banding, knock-down
construction*

Unit 11: Wall Shelf   **47**
Solid wood, edge gluing, veneered panel, *finger
joints, shadow effect*

Unit 12: Bathroom Cabinet   **51**
Plywood, rabbet and dado joints, *sliding doors,* solid
wood trim, painted finish, *composition top material*

SECTION VI: COFFEE TABLES

Unit 13: Modern Coffee Table   **54**
Veneered plywood, solid-maple trim, *decorative spline
joints*

Unit 14: Contemporary Coffee Table   **56**
Edge-to-edge gluing, *mortise/tenon joints, leg notches*

Unit 15: Trestle Coffee Table   **58**
Edge-to-edge gluing, *through mortise,* keyed tenon,
sculptured leg, irregular-distressed edges

Unit 16: Early American Coffee Table   **61**
Edge-to-edge gluing, mortise/tenon joints, *turning,* top
fasteners

SECTION VII: END TABLES

Unit 17: Early American Step Table   **64**
Edge-to-edge joints, mortise/tenon joints, turning,
skeleton frame, *drawer construction,* top fasteners

Unit 18: Pedestal Table   **68**
Enlarging a pattern, *turning,* edge-to-edge joints,
splined miter joints, routing

Unit 19: Modern Corner Table   **71**
Open mortise and tenon, dowel joints, *veneering,* cleats

SECTION VIII: PROJECTS FOR STUDENT PLAN-
NING AND CREATIVITY

Unit 20: Enclosure   **76**
Edge-to-edge gluing, miter joints with cleats, splines,
feathers, rabbetted back

Unit 21: Open Tool Box   78
Edge-to-edge gluing, rabbet joints, plywood bottom in groove, partitions

Unit 22: Box   79
Edge-to-edge gluing, rabbet joints, top cut off after gluing

Unit 23: Display Cabinet   81
Butt, lap, rabbet and dado joints; routing; rabbetted back; small drawers

Unit 24: Chest   83
Edge-to-edge gluing, splined miter joints, veneered panel in groove, decorative legs, top cut off after gluing

Unit 25: Collection Box   85
Rabbet and butt joints, rabbetted back, glass front, front frame with lap joints

Glossary of Wood Furniture Terms   87

APPENDIX I

Metric Equivalents of Fractional Inches   90

APPENDIX II

Inch-Metric/Metric-Inch Conversion Factors   91

Preface

The purpose of this text is to help the student select and plan a variety of wood furniture projects. It is designed for individuals with previous wood shop experience. A detailed, step-by-step approach has been purposely avoided. Instead, each project is presented in a summary manner. The processes, procedures and techniques required to construct specific design and structural features are pointed out. The text also is designed to aid instruction and develop broad experiences in furnituremaking.

PROJECT GROUPINGS

The projects are categorized into functionally related groupings. Two or more furniture styles are included in all groupings. These represent styles and types which are of most interest to students. Each project provides a variety of learning experiences. These are listed in the Table of Contents. Italics are used to indicate special design features which are discussed in more detail.

It is suggested that students study all of the projects in this text. Mastery of basic techniques is necessary for continued development of furnituremaking skills.

MATERIALS

A variety of materials are used in the projects. Open structures are made of solid wood. Large surfaces are constructed from edge-glued pieces. Birch veneered plywood is used to speed case construction. Large items take advantage of the stability and matched grain of plywood. Solid wood trim is used in all case structures. Edge banding is carried out with relatively thin materials. Wider edging is used for shaped and routed edges. Special materials used include veneer, formica, marble and various other composition materials.

FINISH

The appropriate finish for each project is indicated. Discussion is kept to a minimum. Manufacturers' directions are closely followed in all cases.

Wipe-on finishes have been recommended for convenience. Those recommended have been successfully used on all hardwoods. Where appropriate, lacquer is sprayed on to simulate commercial furniture finishes.

STUDENT INVOLVEMENT

This text should stimulate individual activities. The student is shown the type of planning that is needed, and how to enlarge a pattern and develop plans for turning. Construction includes the use of skeleton frames, various drawer assemblies and jointery. Trim activities include routing, facing, and the cutting of special parts.

CONVERSION TO METRIC DIMENSIONING

The dimensions of any of the projects in this text may be converted to metric units of measure. Appendixes in this text list the metric equivalents of fractional inches and provide factors for converting from inch to metric dimensions. Student-planned activities could include the metric dimensioning of some or all of the furniture pieces in one or more projects.

Acknowledgements

Various projects described in this text are the result of student work. I take this opportunity to recognize the following students for their achievements and their contributions: Tom Tugend, Ted Schreiver, Linda Pesch, Walt Fenwick, Bob Drake, Paul McCarthy, John Comerford, Dave Nollar, David Damcott, Mike Bianco, Dave King.

Shop Safety Rules and Practices

Shop accidents involving human injury do *not* 'just happen.' They are caused by *human carelessness*. Failure to observe safe practices and procedures is the most common cause of shop accidents. To prevent injury to yourself and to others, and to avoid needless damage to machines, tools and materials, carefully study the following safety rules. Be sure you understand *all* of the rules, then *practice them at all times in the shop.*

Know the correct procedures for safely operating and using a machine or tool—If you are not absolutely sure that you thoroughly understand how to correctly and safely operate a machine or tool, ask your instructor to explain the procedures and related machine or tool operations.

Observe the following general safety rules related to machine operation:
- Clearly understand the function of each machine control
- Know the correct sequence in which the controls should be used
- Correctly set up the machine *before* turning on the power
- Clear the machine work area of tools, boards and waste material
- Be sure all guards and other safety related devices are in place and are operating correctly
- Be sure the machine is in correct operating condition (cutting surfaces correctly attached and sharp, etc.)
- Know and observe the danger zones on and around the machine
- Maintain a 4-inch margin of safety between your hands and the machine cutting surfaces. (Have push sticks within easy reach, and use them when needed to maintain the safety margin.)
- Permit the machine to come to normal operating speed before using it
- Turn off the machine when cutting operations are completed. (If a brake is provided, use it to stop the cutting surfaces. Never leave an operating machine unattended.)
- Always return the machine cutting surfaces and guides to the normal work position when you have finished. (The normal work position usually is a right-angle orientation.)
- Always wear safety glasses when operating machines. (Also wear earphones and breathing masks or respirators when conditions require them.)
- Wear insulated-sole shoes (not leather) and other appropriately safe clothing. (Secure loose clothing and tie up or cover long hair.)
- Remove all jewelry (rings, watches, necklaces, etc.)

Keep your attention focused on the job you are doing—The safe operation of machines and tools requires the undivided attention of the operator. Do not permit yourself to be distracted. If you must talk to someone or focus your attention away from the job, stop what you are doing, remove the workpiece, and turn off the machine or lay down the tool.

Do not distract others who are operating machines or using tools—If you must talk to someone who is using a machine or tool, wait until they have removed the workpiece from the machine or have finished the tool operation before you attempt to get their attention.

If you observe an unsafe condition or practice, immediately report it to your instructor—Safety is everybody's business and concern.

Drawing Tables

The design features and construction of two general-purpose drawing tables are described in this section. Both tables have medium-size drawing surfaces and can be easily disassembled.

Unit 1: Free-form Drawing Table
Designed to be used while standing, this drawing table features a free-form base, keyed mortise/tenon construction for easy disassembly, and a wooden ratchet mechanism for raising and positioning the drawing surface.

Unit 2: Conventional Drawing Table
Designed to be used while seated, the heavy, utilitarian style of this drawing table features bolted construction for easy disassembly; a large, shallow drawer for storage; and a simple tilt block for holding the drawing surface in a raised position.

1

Fig. 1-1. Free-form drawing table.

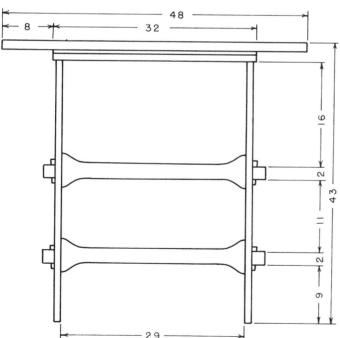

Fig. 1-3. Side view of free-form drawing table, with drawing surface raised and held in position by wooden ratchet mechanism.

Free-Form Drawing Table

The drawing table with free-form base (Fig. 1-1) was designed to be used while standing. Although the design height is 43 inches (Fig. 1-2), the uprights may be shortened to decrease the height.

The base is held securely by keyed *tenons* in the crossrails. The top hinges are attached with screws. This construction allows easy breakdown for moving.

The drawing surface is raised with a wooden *ratchet* mechanism (Fig. 1-3). This is hidden by the ½-inch horizontal spacers when the top is lowered.

BASE PATTERN

Produce a finish-size enlargement of the base pattern in Fig. 1-4. Begin by ruling 1-inch squares on a large piece of wrapping paper. The paper should be at least 42 x 18 inches. Letter the vertical lines in Fig. 1-4. Number the horizontal lines. Place the numbers on the left edge of the pattern in Fig. 1-4. Place corresponding letters and numbers on the full-size pattern. Locate specific grid points in Fig. 1-4 and transfer them to the corresponding locations on the full-size pattern. Use a thin, flexible wood strip to connect the points on the full-size pattern. Cut out the half-pattern.

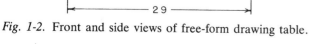

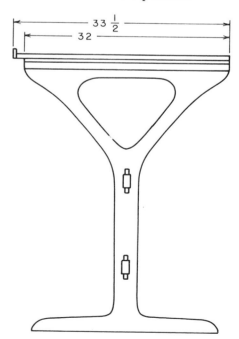

Fig. 1-2. Front and side views of free-form drawing table.

BILL OF MATERIAL
Free-form Drawing Table—Unit 1
(All dimensions are finished size)

Base Parts:
Upper Leg		
Member	2 pc. 1″ x 3″ x 33″	Walnut
Upright	2 pc. 1″ x 4″ x 32″	Walnut
Angles	4 pc. 1″ x 5″ x 26″	Walnut
Foot	2 pc. 1″ x 3″ x 30″	Walnut
Cross Rails	2 pc. 1″ x 5½″ x 35″	Walnut
Keys	4 pc. ½″ x ¾″ x 3″	Walnut

Horizontal Assembly Parts:
Drawing		
Surface	1 pc. ¾″ x 32″ x 46″	Birch Plywood
Facing	2 pc. ¾″ x 1″ x 33″	Walnut
	1 pc. ¾″ x 1″ x 48″	Walnut
Pencil		
Strip	1 pc. ½″ x 1½″ x 48″	Walnut
Frame		
Members	4 pc. 1″ x 1½″ x 32″	Walnut
Spacers	4 pc. ½″ x 1½″ x 32″	Walnut
Ratchet	2 pc. 1″ x 1½″ x 29″	Walnut
Dowel Pins	8 pc. ⅜″ x 2″	Birch
Screws	6 pc. Flat Head, 2½″ #8	

Raising Assembly Parts:
Leg	2 pc. ½″ x 1½″ x 15″	Walnut
Cross		
Members	3 pc. ½″ x 1½″ x 29″	Walnut
Hinges	4 pc. 2″ Butt	Brass
Screws	5 pc. Flat Head, 1″ #8	

BASE CONSTRUCTION

Mill the base stock to the sizes specified in the *Bill of Material*. Cut and glue the 80-degree miter joint which forms the leg-support (Fig. 1-5). Allow the glue to set before proceeding.

Construct a fixture (Fig. 1-6) to secure the leg-support joints

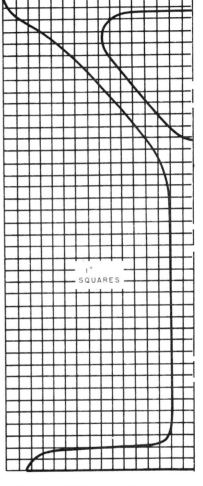

Fig. 1-4. Half-pattern for the base.

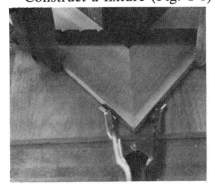

Fig. 1-5. Clamping of the 80-degree miter joint which forms the leg-support triangle.

Fig. 1-6. Fixture used to secure the leg-support joints during cutting.

while they are being cut. The fixture consists of two cleats on a square board. Accurately position the cleats at the correct angle and secure them with screws. Position the screws so they will not interfere with the saw cuts.

Cut a lap joint in the angle formed by the leg joints (Fig. 1-7).

Fig. 1-7. Leg support held in a fixture during cutting of the lap joint.

Fig. 1-8. The point of the leg support is cut off after the lap joint is cut, as shown here.

Fig. 1-9. The fixture is turned 90 degrees and used to secure the leg support during lapping of the upper corners.

Use a dado head on the radial arm saw for this and all lap joints. Cut off the point of the leg-support joint (Fig. 1-8).

Turn the fixture 90 degrees and prepare to cut lap joints on the upper corners of the leg-support triangle (Fig. 1-9). First, remove the unneeded cleat from the fixture. Next, apply abrasive paper to the fixture to help hold the workpiece. Position the workpiece in the fixture and place a brad in the waste edge of the workpiece. The fixture supports the workpiece which extends over the fence.

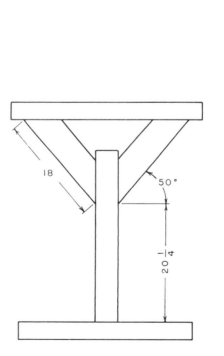

Fig. 1-10. Side view of the free-form leg assembly.

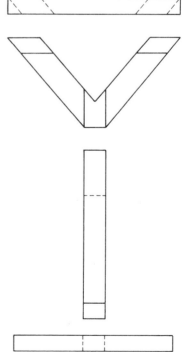

Fig. 1-11. Side view of the leg assembly showing lap joints.

Correctly locate and cut lap joints on the upper corners of the leg-support triangle (Fig. 1-9) and then on the cross member (Figs. 1-10 and 1-11). Next, cut lap joints on the upright and the foot.

Glue and clamp the leg assembly. Use parallel clamps and pressure blocks to distribute pressure evenly over each joint surface. No further fitting is necessary if the joints are cut accurately. (If desired, a trial assembly made of poplar can be constructed first.)

Fig. 1-12. Correct placement of the pattern on the leg assembly.

Fig. 1-13. Close-up view showing correct pattern placement on the upper leg assembly.

Fig. 1-14. Close-up view of the upper leg assembly showing the layout lines.

Place the previously prepared pattern on the leg assembly and trace around it. See Figs. 1-12, 1-13 and 1-14. Cut around the layout lines with the band saw and jigsaw. Create the free-form shape (Fig. 1-15) with surform files, spokeshave and similar hand tools.

Cut the *mortise* for the crossrails. Sand the leg assemblies to finished shape.

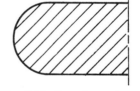

Fig. 1-15. Free-form shape.

CROSSRAIL CONSTRUCTION

Develop a finish-size pattern for the crossrails using the pattern in Fig. 1-16. Cut around the layout lines with a band saw. Hand shape the *tenons* to fit the 1 x 2-inch mortises in the legs. Cut an opening in each tenon for the mortise key. Adjust the shape and size of the keys to tightly wedge the base assembly. Cut and sand them to final shape.

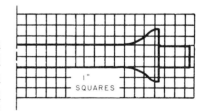

Fig. 1-16. Pattern for the crossrails.

HORIZONTAL ASSEMBLY CONSTRUCTION

Cut the parts for the *horizontal assembly* as specified in the *Bill of Materials*. Miter the corners of the frame members and spacers.

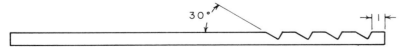

Fig. 1-17. Rachet strip of the raising mechanism.

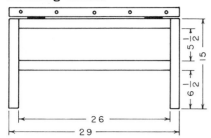

Fig. 1-18. The raising mechanism is attached to the underside of the drawing surface.

Assemble the frame with dowels. Use two dowels at each corner. Glue ½-inch spacers on the top of this assembly. Cut notches on the ratchet strips with the band saw (Fig. 1-17). Edge glue the ratchet strips inside the 1-inch frame.

TOP CONSTRUCTION

Smooth the drawing surface edges with the jointer. Apply walnut facing on the two sides and the front. The facing should be edge glued, with miter joints at the *front* corners. Joint the remaining plywood edge and the facing ends. Edge glue the pencil strip to the lower edge.

Construct the raising mechanism with lap joints (Fig. 1-18). Position and attach the hinges on the raising mechanism. Attach the other sides of the hinges with screws to the underside of the drawing surface. The hinge line is 18 inches from the top edge.

Place hinges on the back edge of the drawing surface. Position the hinges to provide a 1½-inch overhang from the pencil strip to the lower frame. Attach the horizontal assembly hinges to the base with screws.

SURFACE FINISHING

Perform final sanding of the table, and finish it with Danish oil.

UNIT 2
Conventional Drawing Table

The conventional drawing table in Fig. 2-1 was designed to be used while seated. The height is 36 inches (Fig. 2-2). The lower crossrail is designed to function as a footrest. A large, shallow drawer (Fig. 2-3) is included for drawings and drafting supplies. Although the bolted construction makes disassembly easy, the table is extremely sturdy.

BASE CONSTRUCTION

Cut parts for the legs as specified in the *Bill of Material* and in Fig. 2-4. The legs and feet are permanently assembled by means of three evenly spaced dowels. The dimensions of these workpieces assure a ¼-inch shoulder around the base of the legs (Fig. 2-5). Drill the upper leg members and attach with 2½-inch machine bolts.

The cross rails are fabricated to allow assembly with 4-inch machine bolts (Fig. 2-6). Matching holes should be drilled for the dowels, after drilling and placing the bolts. The dowel holes should be positioned with dowel centers to assure a perfect fit. Mated parts should be identified. The dowels are glued in the crossrails and protrude ½ inch. These prevent the crossrails from rotating.

Drawer runners should be screwed on the inside of the legs. Place them ½ inch from the top. Construction of the base is completed by screwing the horizontal surface in place. Glides may be placed under the feet.

TOP CONSTRUCTION

Smooth the edges of the drawing surface on the jointer. Face the front and the two sides of the drawing surface with hard maple.

Fig. 2-1. Conventional drawing table.

Fig. 2-3. Features of the conventional drawing table include bolted construction and a large, shallow drawer.

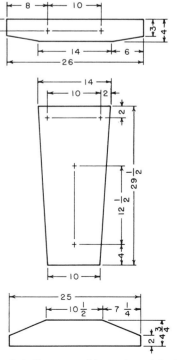

Fig. 2-4. Leg assembly parts and their dimensions.

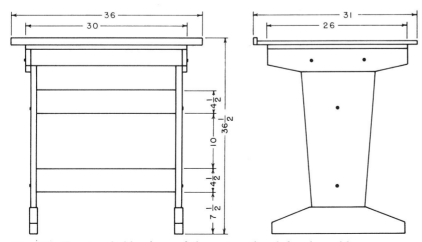

Fig. 2-2. Front and side views of the conventional drawing table.

Fig. 2-5. Base of the leg assembly.

BILL OF MATERIAL
Conventional Drawing Table—Unit 2
(All dimensions are finished size)

Base Parts:

Leg	2 pc. 1″ x 14″ x 29½″	Maple
Foot	2 pc. 1½″ x 4¾″ x 25″	Maple
Cross Rail	2 pc. 1″ x 4½″ x 26″	Maple
Upper Leg Member	2 pc. 1″ x 4″ x 26″	Maple
Horizontal Surface	1 pc. ¾″ x 26″ x 30″	Birch Plywood
Drawer Runners	2 pc. ¾″ x 1″ x 14″	Maple
Dowels	6 pc. ⅜″ x 2½″	Birch
	4 pc. ⅜″ x 2″	Birch
Bolts	4 pc. ⅜″ x 2½″	
	4 pc. ⅜″ x 4″	
Screws	12 pc. Flat Head, 1½″, #10	
Cushion Glides	4 pc.	

Top Parts:

Drawing Surface	1 pc. ¾″ x 29½″ x 34″	Birch Plywood
Facing	2 pc. ¾″ x 1″ x 30½″	Maple
	1 pc. ¾″ x 1″ x 36″	Maple
Pencil Strip	1 pc. ½″ x 1¼″ x 36″	Maple
Tilt Block	1 pc. 1¼″ x 3¼″ x 30″	Spruce

Drawer Parts:

Front	1 pc. ¾″ x 3″ x 28″	Maple
Sides	2 pc. ¾″ x 3″ x 24″	Poplar
Back	1 pc. ¾″ x 3″ x 23¾″	Poplar
Bottom	1 pc. ¼″ x 23″ x 23½″	Fir Plywood

The facing should be edge glued, with miter joints at the front corners. Joint the remaining edge of the plywood and the facing ends. Edge glue the pencil strip along the lower edge.

Hinges are screwed on the underside of the drawing surface. Position them to provide a 2½-inch overhang from the pencil strip to the lower plywood.

Machine a simple tilt block to raise the top (Fig. 2-7). Cut a 15-degree angle on one edge of the tilt block.

DRAWER CONSTRUCTION

The drawer is constructed last so that it can be accurately fitted to the table. The material used for the drawer is ¾-inch thick (Fig. 2-8). Use dado joints for strength.

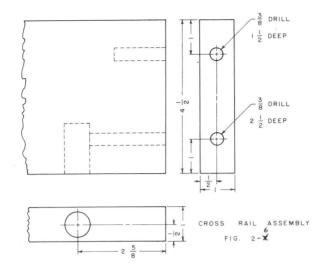

Fig. 2-6. Views of the crossrail end showing the dowel and bolt hole locations.

Fig. 2-7. Side view of conventional drawing table with drawing surface raised.

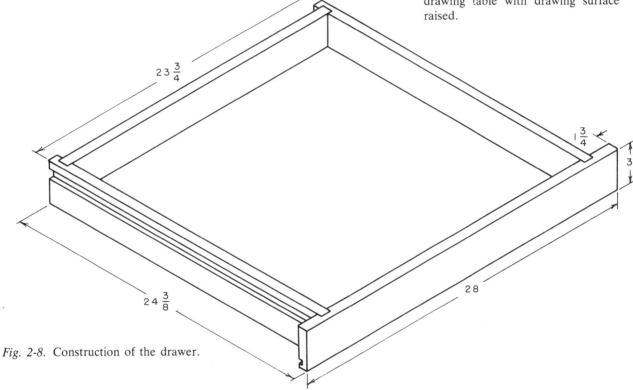

Fig. 2-8. Construction of the drawer.

Slightly enlarge the groove for the drawer runner. This will allow the drawer to slide easily. Space the groove so that the drawer will hang slightly below the upper leg members. All joints should be cut ⅜-inch deep.

The drawer bottom is made of ¼-inch plywood. Space the bottom grooves ¼ inch up from the lower edge. Fit the complete drawer to the table, then assemble with glue and finish nails.

SURFACE FINISH

Thoroughly sand the drawing table, and finish it with several coats of Danish oil.

SECTION II
Three-Drawer Chests

The design features and construction of three styles of three-drawer chests are described in this section. The case of each is constructed of skeleton frames and solid ends. The drawers are of simple box construction. Each chest is designed for a specific purpose and decor, which dictates the overall size, trim type and surface finish.

Unit 3:
Three-Drawer Dresser

This Early American design features sculptured feet, large drawers with metal side guides, and a sprayed lacquer finish.

Unit 4: Three-Drawer Chest

The relatively simple style and moderate size of this chest fit most settings. Its features include a solid base, maple facing and trim, and medium-size drawers with wooden center guides.

Unit 5: Three-Drawer Dresser

This distinctive design features panel-and-frame construction with cherry veneer inset panels in the ends, wide front facings of solid cherry, and a solid cherry top.

Fig. 3-1. Three-drawer dresser.

UNIT 3
Three-Drawer Dresser

The style of the large three-drawer dresser in Fig. 3-1 is Early American. The trim and sculptured feet match existing furniture. The design (Fig. 3-2) features large drawers. Metal side guides are used to support the drawer weight. The dresser is finished with sprayed lacquer.

CASE CONSTRUCTION

Cut the rails and stiles for the skeleton frame (Fig. 3-3) as specified in the *Bill of Material.* Cut a ¼ x ⅜-inch groove in one edge of each rail. While holding the stiles upright in a fixture (Fig. 3-4), cut a ¼ x ⅜-inch groove in both ends. (If a dust panel between the drawers is desired, also cut a ¼ x ⅜-inch groove along one edge of each stile.)

Glue and assemble the rails and stiles with splines. Clamp each assembled frame and allow it to lay flat while the glue dries.

Cut the ends of the case to size. Smooth the edges on a jointer. Lay out and cut in the case ends the ⅜-inch-deep dado joints for the skeleton frames (Fig. 3-5). To prevent chipping the birch veneered surface, make the cuts with a dado head on the radial arm saw. Cuts are to be made from both edges. With the table saw, cut ¼ x ⅜-inch rabbets on the back edges.

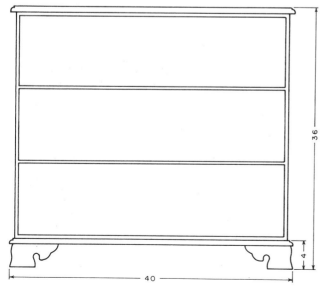

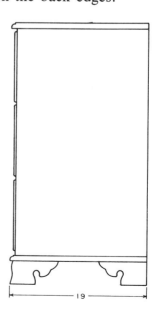

Fig. 3-2. Front and side views of the three-drawer dresser.

BILL OF MATERIAL
Three-Drawer Dresser—Unit 3
(All dimensions are finished size)

Case Parts:

Ends	2 pc. ¾″ x 18″ x 31¼″	Birch Plywood
Skeleton Frame	8 pc. ¾″ x 2″ x 37¾″	Poplar
	8 pc. ¾″ x 2″ x 13¾″	Poplar
Splines	16 pc. ¼″ x ¾″ x 2″	Fir Plywood
Facing	4 pc. ¼″ x ¾″ x 37″	Maple
	2 pc. ¼″ x ¾″ x 31¼″	Maple
Back	1 pc. ¼″ x 31¼″ x 37¾″	Fir Plywood
Top	1 pc. ¾″ x 18¼″ x 38½″	Birch Plywood
Top Facing	1 pc. ¾″ x ¾″ x 40″	Maple
	2 pc. ¾″ x ¾″ x 19″	Maple
Base Apron	1 pc. ¾″ x 1¾″ x 40″	Maple
	1 pc. ¾″ x 1¾″ x 36½″	Maple
	2 pc. ¾″ x 1¾″ x 19″	Maple
Feet	8 pc. ¾″ x 3¼″ x 6½″	Maple
Corner Blocks	4 pc. 1¼″ x 1¼″ x 3″	Poplar
Cleats	8 pc. ¾″ x ¾″ x 3¼″	Poplar
Screws	32 pc. Flat Head, 1¼″, #8	
Side Guides	3 pr.	

Drawer Parts:

Sides	6 pc. ½″ x 9″ x 17″	Poplar
Front and Back	6 pc. ½″ x 9″ x 35½″	Poplar
Bottom	3 pc. ¼″ x 16½″ x 35½″	Fir Plywood
Decorative Fronts	3 pc. ½″ x 9¹⁵/₁₆″ x 37½″	Maple
Screws	18 pc. Flat Head, ¾″ x #8	
Handles	6 pc. Antique Brass	

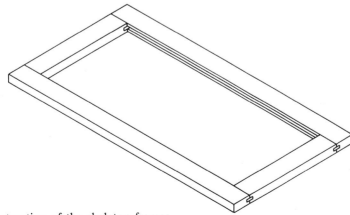

Fig. 3-4. The stiles should be held upright in a fixture when grooves are cut in their ends.

Fig. 3-3. Construction of the skeleton frames.

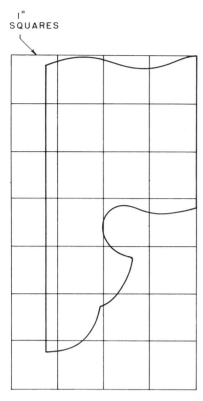

1"
SQUARES

Fig. 3-6. Pattern for the sculptured feet.

Before gluing the case ends and skeleton frames, perform a trial assembly. If the parts fit correctly, glue and assemble them. Use bar clamps to hold the assembly until the glue sets.

Cut the ¼-inch maple facing for the cabinet front. Attach it with glue and brads.

Machine the material for the apron, and then shape it with a ⅜ rounding over bit in the router shaper table. Raise the bit to create the square shoulder below the round. After machining, miter the front corners. Cut the pieces to fit and then drill the screw holes. The apron should extend out ¾ inch from the cabinet sides and front. The rear corners and the back piece should be square and flush with the case frame. Attach the apron to the case bottom with screws.

FEET CONSTRUCTION

Prepare to make a cove cut on the single piece of stock from which six of the feet later will be cut. (The material for the two back foot pieces is left flat.) Clamp a fence at a 50-degree angle behind the table saw blade. Pass the workpiece sideways over the blade. Start with the blade barely protruding. Take successively deeper cuts until a ¼-inch-deep cove is completed. Cut the upper edge with the router. Finish the material to the basic shape with a hand plane.

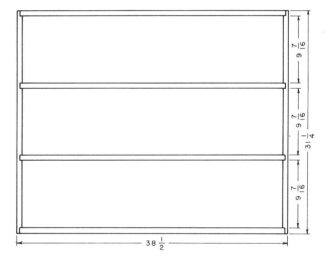

Fig. 3-5. Construction of the case.

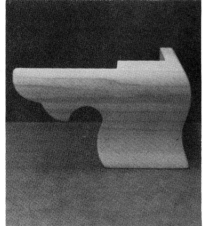

Fig. 3-7. Design and construction of the sculptured feet.

Cut the workpiece into individual foot pieces. Cut the foot pieces in pairs, with mitered corners on the four front foot pieces. The back foot pieces are cut square.

Prepare a finish-size enlargement of the foot pattern in Fig. 3-6. Place it on each foot piece and trace around it. Cut out on the band saw and then sand.

Assemble the feet by gluing them together with glue blocks. Use parallel clamps to hold the pieces until the glue sets. The back feet have one sculptured piece and one flat piece. Attach cleats to the upper edges of the feet with screws. Sand the joined pieces to complete the basic cross section (Fig. 3-7). Attach the feet to the cabinet apron with screws.

Cut the top surface from birch plywood. Smooth the edges on a jointer. Cut the top facing to fit, with miter joints on the front. Edge glue the facing to the top. Shape the facing edges the same as the lower apron, but with a hand-held router. Drill holes in the top skeleton frame, and attach the top to it with screws.

DRAWER CONSTRUCTION

Machine the material for the drawers. As shown in Fig. 3-8, the drawer design is a simple box construction. Note that a 1-inch allowance is made for the metal side guides. Place a groove ¼ inch up from the edges of all pieces. Cut a ½-inch rabbet joint on each end of the sides. Cut and fit the bottom. Glue and assemble the drawers with finish nails.

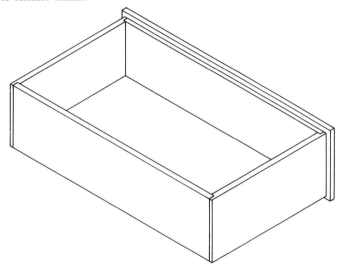

Fig. 3-8. Simple box construction of the drawers.

Cut the pieces for the decorative drawer fronts. Shape the edges with a ¼ rounding over bit in the router. Properly position the decorative fronts on the drawers. The design provides a ¼-inch lap on all edges. Drill and attach the fronts with screws.

FINISHING

Install the metal drawer guides according to the manufacturer's directions. Cut and attach the cabinet back with brads. Sand the dresser, then apply stain and the spray lacquer. When the lacquer is dry, install the handles.

Fig. 4-1. Three-drawer chest.

Three-Drawer Chest

The plain style of the three-drawer chest in Fig. 4-1 will fit in any setting. The overall size (Fig. 4-2) permits use in any room. The large drawers provide generous storage.

CASE CONSTRUCTION

Cut the rails and stiles for the skeleton frames (Fig. 4-3) as specified in the *Bill of Material*. Cut a ¼ x ⅜-inch groove along one edge of each rail. Cut identical grooves in both ends of the stiles. Hold the pieces upright in a fixture when cutting the grooves (Fig. 4-4). (If a dust panel between drawers is desired, cut a ¼ x ⅜-inch groove along one edge of each stile.) Glue and assemble the skeleton frames with splines. Clamp the frames and lay them on a flat surface while the glue sets.

Cut the ends for the case (Fig. 4-5). Smooth the edges on the jointer. Lay out and cut ⅜-inch-deep dado joints for the skeleton frames. Use a dado head on the radial arm saw. This eliminates chipping of the birch veneered surface. The cuts should be made

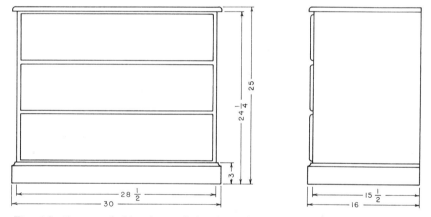

Fig. 4-2. Front and side views of the three-drawer chest.

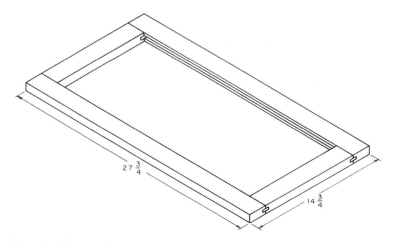

Fig. 4-3. Construction of the skeleton frames.

16

BILL OF MATERIAL
Three-Drawer Chest—Unit 4
(All dimensions are finished size)

Case Parts:

Ends	2 pc. ¾″ x 15″ x 24¼″	Birch Plywood
Skeleton Frames	8 pc. ¾″ x 2″ x 27¾″	Poplar
	8 pc. ¾″ x 2″ x 10¾″	Poplar
Splines	16 pc. ¼″ x ¾″ x 2″	Fir Plywood
Facing	4 pc. ¼″ x ¾″ x 27″	Maple
	2 pc. ¼″ x ¾″ x 24¼″	Maple
Back	1 pc. ¼″ x 21¾″ x 27¾″	Fir Plywood
Top	1 pc. ¾″ x 15¼″ x 28½″	Birch Plywod
Top Facing	1 pc. ¾″ x ¾″x 30″	Maple
	2 pc. ¾″ x ¾″ x 16″	Maple
Base Trim	1 pc. ¾″ x 3″ x 30″	Maple
	2 pc. ¾″ x 3″ x 16″	Maple
Screws	8 pc. Flat Head, 1¼″, #8	

Fig. 4-4. Stiles should be held upright in a fixture while the grooves are cut in their ends.

Drawer parts:

Sides	6 pc. ½″ x 6″ x 14″	Poplar
Front and Back	6 pc. ½″ x 6″ x 26¼″	Poplar
Bottom	3 pc. ¼″ x 13½″ x 26¼″	Fir Plywood
Decorative Front	3 pc. ½″ x 6½″ x 27½″	Maple
Drawer Runner	6 pc. ¼″ x 1″ x 13″	Poplar
Center Guide	3 pc. ¾″ x ¾″ x 14¾″	Poplar
Screws	18 pc. Flat Head, ¾″, #8	
Handles	6 pc. Antique Brass	

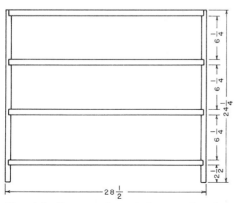

Fig. 4-5. Construction of the case for the three-drawer chest.

Fig. 4-6. The base trim should be glued and clamped to the case as shown here.

Fig. 4-7. The bottom rail should extend ¼ inch above the base trim.

from both edges. Use the table saw to cut a ¼ x ⅜-inch rabbet on the back edges.

Carry out a trial assembly before gluing the case ends and skeleton frames. If the pieces fit properly, glue and assemble them with bar clamps. (Note that the case ends extend to the floor. This aids in attaching the base trim.)

Cut the ¼-inch maple facing for the case front. Attach the facing with glue and brads.

Cut the material for the base trim. Use a router and ⅜ cove bit to shape the upper edge. Cut the trim to fit the base, with miter joints at the front corners. Glue the trim to the surfaces of the case and clamp as shown in Fig. 4-6. The bottom rail should extend ¼ inch above the base trim (Fig. 4-7).

Cut the birch plywood top. Smooth the edges on the jointer. Cut the top facing and edge glue it to the top. Use miter joints at the front corners. Use a hand-held router and a ⅜ rounding over bit to shape the edge of the top facing. Lower the bit to create the square edge above the round. Attach the top to the case with screws.

DRAWER CONSTRUCTION

Cut the material for the drawers. The drawer design is a simple box construction (Fig. 4-8). Place a groove ¼ inch up from the edge of the side, back and front pieces. Cut ½-inch rabbet joints on the ends of the side pieces. Cut and fit the bottom piece. Glue and assemble the drawers with finish nails.

Position the drawer runners on the bottom of the drawer. Allow ¹³⁄₁₆ inch between the runners for the center guide. Glue and hold the runners in place until the glue sets. Notch the back edge of the drawer between the runners.

Fabricate the drawer center guides (Fig. 4-9). To correctly position each guide, center each drawer in its case opening. Carefully remove the drawer without disturbing the guide. Glue and clamp each guide in the skeleton frame.

Cut the decorative drawer fronts. Shape their edges with a ¼

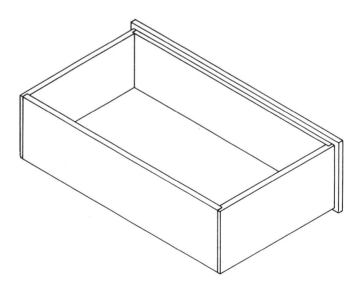

Fig. 4-8. Simple box construction of the drawers.

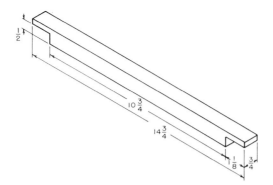

Fig. 4-9. The drawer center guide design.

rounding over bit in the router. Correctly position the decorative drawer fronts so that their bottom edges just cover the rail below them. A ¼-inch lap is provided on all other edges. Drill and attach the decorative fronts with screws. Attach the cabinet back to the case with brads.

FINISHING

Thoroughly sand the chest and then apply stain. Spray on two coats of lacquer sealer and then two coats of dull-gloss lacquer. When the lacquer has dried, install the handles.

Fig. 5-1. Three-drawer dresser.

Fig. 5-3. The dresser ends are constructed of solid cherry frames and cherry veneered hardboard inset panels.

Three-Drawer Dresser

The three-drawer dresser in Fig. 5-1 features cherry veneer inset panels in the ends and wide front facings of solid cherry. The overall dimensions of the dresser are shown in Fig. 5-2.

VENEERED PANEL FABRICATION

Select the cherry veneer for the end inset panels (Fig. 5-3). Both the face and the back of the ¼-inch hardboard should be veneered, to assure a stable workpiece. The inset panels should be made slightly oversize and later trimmed to the finished size.

Clamp the veneer between plywood (Fig. 5-4) and joint the edges on the jointer. Tape the veneer splices and splits with brown paper tape. (Do *not* use masking tape. Pressure would force the masking tape into the wood pores.) For easy removal later, place the tape on the *outside* surfaces of the veneer.

Attach the veneer to the hardboard front and back surfaces with plastic resin glue. If a means of applying pressure is not available, use contact cement.

The correct mixture of resin glue and water depends on the number of square feet to be covered. Use 12.5 grams of glue and 7.5 grams of water per square foot. In this case, there are eight 1.3 square-foot surfaces, producing a total of 10.4 square feet. The correct amount of glue therefore is (12.5 grams x 10.4), or 130 grams. The correct amount of water is (7.5 grams x 10.4), or 78 grams.

Mix the water and glue, a little at a time. When the water and glue are thoroughly mixed, brush the mixture on the hardboard

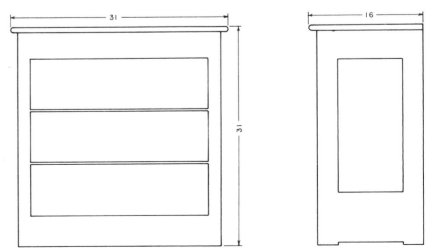

Fig. 5-2. Front and side views of the three-drawer dresser.

20

BILL OF MATERIAL
Three-Drawer Dresser—Unit 5
(All dimensions are finished size)

Three-Drawer Dresser

Fig. 5-4. Clamp the veneer between plywood when jointing the edges.

End Parts:

Top Stile	2 pc. ¾″ x 4″ x 9″	Cherry
Bottom Stile	2 pc. ¾″ x 7″ x 9″	Cherry
Back Rail	2 pc. ¾″ x 3″ x 30¼″	Cherry
Front Rail	2 pc. ¾″ x 2¼″ x 30¼″	Cherry
Inset Panel	2 pc. ¼″ x 9½″ x 19¼″	Hardboard
	4 pc. 9½″ x 19¼″	Cherry Veneer
Spline Material	1 pc. ¾″ x 7″ x 10″	Cherry

Case Parts:

Skeleton Frames	8 pc. ¾″ x 2″ x 28″	Poplar
	8 pc. ¾″ x 2″ x 10″	Poplar
Spline	16 pc. ¼″ x ¾″ x 2″	Fir Plywood

Facing (Front):

Sides	2 pc. ¾″ x 2″ x 30¼″	Cherry
Top	1 pc. ¾″ x 4″ x 25″	Cherry
Center	2 pc. ¾″ x ¾″ x 25″	Cherry
Bottom	1 pc. ¾″ x 4½″ x 25″	Cherry
Dowels	12 pc. ⅜″ x 2½″	Dowel Pin
Top	1 pc. ¾″ x 16″ x 31″	Cherry
Cleats	1 pc. ¾″ x ¾″ x 26″	Poplar
	2 pc. ¾″ x ¾″ x 12″	Poplar
Back	1 pc. ¼″ x 26½″ x 28″	Fir Plywood

Drawer Parts:

Sides	6 pc. ½″ x 6½″ x 14″	Poplar
Front and Back	6 pc. ½″ x 6½″ x 24¼″	Poplar
Bottom	3 pc. ¼″ x 13½″ x 24¼″	Fir Plywod
Decorative Fronts	3 pc. ½″ x 7¼″ x 25½″	Cherry
Drawer Runners	6 pc. ¼″ x 1″ x 13″	Poplar
Center Guide	3 pc. ¾″ x ¾″ x 14″	Poplar
Pulls	6 pc.	Round Wood

surfaces and on the *back* surfaces of the veneer. Apply enough of the mixture to make the surfaces appear well wetted. Position the veneer on the hardboard and apply pressure. Allow sufficient drying time. After drying is complete, trim the veneered insets to finish size. Carefully scrape off the tape and sand the surfaces.

21

Fig. 5-6. The stiles should be held upright in a fixture when the grooves are cut in their ends.

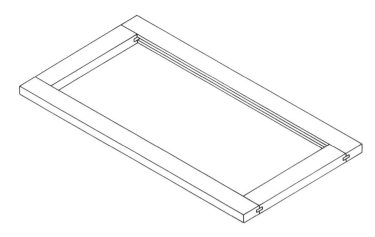

Fig. 5-5. Construction of the skeleton frames.

CASE CONSTRUCTION

Cut the materials for the end frames as specified in the *Bill of Material.* Machine a ¼-inch-deep groove along one edge of the stiles and rails. Cut an identical groove in the ends of the stiles. Measure the thickness of the inset panel to determine the groove width needed for easy fitting of the panel. Plane the ¾-inch board for the splines to the thickness needed to fit the grooves in the rails and stiles. Cut ½-inch-wide splines, with the grain perpendicular to the long edge. Perform a trial assembly to check the fit of the end pieces. Note that the base stile is ½ inch above the rail bottom edges. Glue and clamp the end pieces.

Cut the rails and stiles for the skeleton frames (Fig. 5-5) as specified in the *Bill of Material.* Cut a ¼ x ⅜-inch groove along one edge of each rail. Cut identical grooves in both ends of the stiles. Hold the pieces upright in a fixture when cutting the grooves in the ends (Fig. 5-6). If a dust cover between drawers is desired, cut a ¼ x ⅜-inch groove along one edge of each stile. Glue and assemble the skeleton frames and lay them on a flat surface while the glue sets.

Lay out and cut ¼-inch-deep dado joints on the inside of the end panels (Fig. 5-7). Use a dado head on the radial arm saw. Cuts

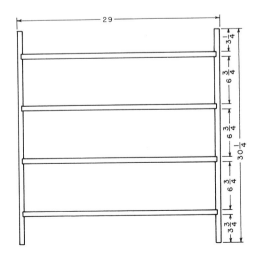

Fig. 5-7. Construction of the case.

should be made from both edges. Use the table saw to cut ¼ x ⅜-inch rabbets on the back edges of the end panels.

Perform a trial assembly before gluing the ends to the skeleton frames. If the pieces fit correctly, glue and assemble them with bar clamps. Use pressure boards across the ends. Do not damage the end joints when applying pressure.

Cut the ¾-inch cherry front facing pieces. Carefully cut the pieces to fit the front of the case. Layout holes for the dowel joints. Use a dowel-it jig to drill the dowel holes. Use ⅜ x 2½-inch dowel pins. Glue and clamp the facing assembly. Attach the facing to the cabinet face with finish nails (Fig. 5-8).

Select the material for the top. Prepare it for edge-to-edge gluing of the surface. Plane and cut the top to finished size. Shape the edges with a ⅜ rounding over bit in a hand-held router. Shape the bottom and top of the front and sides. Attach the top to the front facing and ends with cleats.

Fig. 5-8. Completed case with the front facing attached.

DRAWER CONSTRUCTION

Cut the material for the drawers (Fig. 5-9). Cut a groove ¼ inch up from the bottom edge of all pieces. Cut ½-inch rabbet joints on the ends of the sides. Cut and fit the bottom. Glue and assemble the drawers with finish nails.

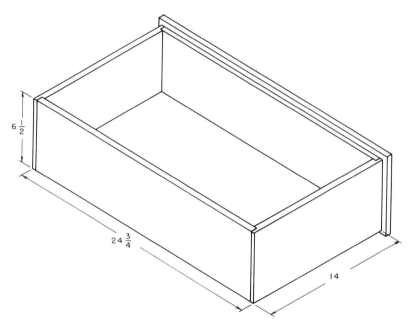

Fig. 5-9. Simple box construction of the drawers.

Cut and position the runners on the bottom of the drawers. Leave a ¹³/₁₆-inch space between the runners for the center guide. Glue and hold the runners in place. Cut a notch in the back edge of the drawer between the runners.

Fabricate the center guide (Fig. 5-10). Cut notches in the ends to fit the skeleton frame. Position the guides by centering each drawer in its case opening. Carefully remove the drawer without disturbing the guide. Glue the guide in the skeleton frame.

Cut the decorative drawer fronts. Shape the edges with a ¼ rounding over bit in the router. Correctly position the decorative

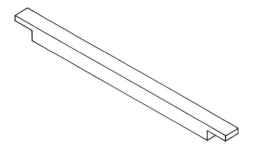

Fig. 5-10. Design of the drawer center guides.

fronts on the drawers. There should be a ¼-inch lap between the drawer and all edges of the decorative front. Drill and attach the decorative fronts to the drawers with screws.

FINISHING

Cut and attach the cabinet back with brads. Thoroughly sand the cabinet surfaces. Apply a Danish oil finish. Install the drawer pulls.

SECTION III

Hope Chests

The design features and construction of two contrasting styles of hope chests are described in this section.

Unit 6: Utility Hope Chest

This plainly styled chest is relatively small and easy to construct. The major structural pieces are cut from birch plywood and are mated with rabbet and dado joints. The joints are covered with simple, L-shaped trim. The feet are integral parts of the structure. No ornate trim or scalloped pieces are required.

Unit 7: Early American Hope Chest

Ornate, decorative trim is a distinctive feature of this relatively large chest. Decorative drawer fronts and scalloped base and top trim establish the Early American style. Compound miter joints are used to mate the top trim pieces. The major structural pieces are cut from birch plywood and are mated with splined miter joints. The large size and ornate trim make this chest a dominant furniture piece.

Fig. 6-1. Utility hope chest.

UNIT 6
Utility Hope Chest

The simple style and moderate size of the utility hope chest in Fig. 6-1 make it suitable for any setting. The chest can be used for convenient storage of clothes, linens, games, records or similar items. The basic structure (Fig. 6-2) is made with rabbet and dado joints. The top and base trim is mitered.

CONSTRUCTION

Cut the workpieces for the front, back, ends and top from birch plywood as specified in the *Bill of Material.* Rip the material to the required width on the table saw. Perform crosscuts on the radial arm saw, to avoid chipping. Cuts will be made from both edges. Be sure the grain on the end pieces runs parallel to the shortest dimension of the workpiece.

Prepare to cut ⅜ x ¾-inch rabbet joints on the ends of the front and back pieces. These should be cut on the table saw. First, register the workpiece end against the fence with an auxiliary board. The initial cut for each rabbet joint should be made with a crosscut blade. Shear the veneer surface ¾ inch from the workpiece end. Install a ¾ dado head in the saw and place it against the fence. Use the dado to clean out the joint. Cut a ⅜ x ¾-inch groove for the bottom along one edge of the front, back and end pieces. Place the grooves 4 inches from the lower edge.

Lay out the feet on all workpieces (Fig. 6-3). Measure 3¾ inches in from the ends of the front and back pieces. Measure 3⅜ inches in from the ends of the end pieces. The length of each foot totals 4 inches, including the trim and the joint. Use the table saw to cut the straight area between the feet. First, set the fence 2½ inches from the blade. Then, raise the blade through each piece and move the piece forward. Cut the curves with a band saw and sand them to finished shape with a spindle sander.

Perform a trail assembly of the major workpieces with the bottom in place. If the major pieces fit correctly, glue the rabbet

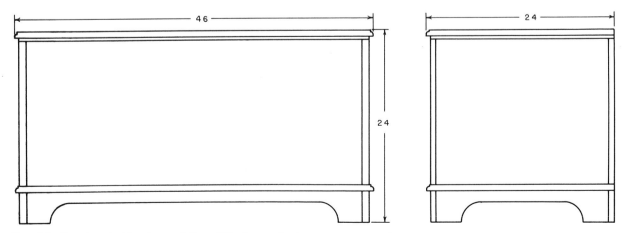

Fig. 6-2. Front and side views of the utility hope chest.

BILL OF MATERIAL
Utility Hope Chest—Unit 6
(All dimensions are finished size)

Front and		
Back	2 pc. ¾″ x 23″ x 44½″	Birch Plywood
End	2 pc. ¾″ x 23″ x 22½″	Birch Plywood
Bottom	1 pc. ¾″ x 21¾″ x 43¾″	Fir Plywood
Top	1 pc. ¾″ x 23¼″ x 44½″	Birch Plywood
Trim	2 pc. ¾″ x ¾″ x 46″	Maple
	4 pc. ¾″ x ¾″ x 24″	Maple
L-shaped		
Trim	1 pc. ¾″ x 1″ x 45″	Maple
	2 pc. ¾″ x 1″ x 23½″	Maple
	2 pc. ¾″ x 1″ x 17¾″	Maple
	2 pc. ¾″ x 1″ x 4″	Maple
Facing	1 pc. ¼″ x ¾″ x 43″	Maple
	2 pc. ¼″ x ¾″ x 17¾″	Maple
	2 pc. ¼″ x ¾″ x 4″	Maple
Piano		
Hinge	1 pc. 1½″ x 43″	
Lid		
Support	2 pc.	

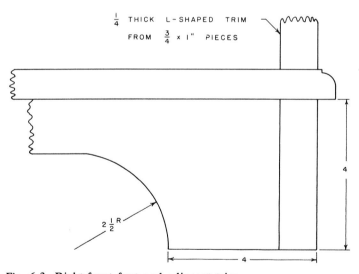

Fig. 6-3. Right-front foot and adjacent trim.

joints and assemble the unit with finish nails.

Machine the L-shaped trim for the edges and the corners. Cut the ¾ x 1-inch trim stock on the table saw to make a ¼-inch-thick L-shape. Make two cuts at right angles to each other.

Cut the L-shaped pieces for the top edges of the chest to finished size. Fit each piece, with 45-degree miters at the front corners. Glue the pieces and clamp them in position.

Machine the trim for the base of the chest. Install a router in the router/shaper table. Use a ⅜ rounding over bit. Raise the bit to produce the square edge below the round on the trim (Fig. 6-3). Cut the base trim to length, with 45-degree miters at the front corners. Glue the pieces and clamp them in position.

Cut the remaining L-shaped trim to fit the front corners and the front legs. Glue the pieces and clamp them in position.

Machine the ¼ x ¾-inch facing for the back edges of the chest. Use it to cover the rabbet joints on the back corners and legs. Glue the pieces and attach them with brads. (The facing piece on the back edge may be planed thinner to make a gain for the piano hinge.)

Cut the birch plywood top. Smooth the edges on the jointer. Cut the ¾ x ¾-inch trim to fit, with miters at the front corners. Glue the pieces and clamp them in position. Use a hand-held router to shape the trim to match that on the base.

FINISHING

Thoroughly sand the chest. Apply Early American brown stain. Finish with antique oil. Commercial cedar lining may be applied to the chest interior, if desired. Attach the top with the piano hinge, then install the lid-support mechanism and related hardware.

UNIT 7

EARLY AMERICAN HOPE CHEST

Fig. 7-1. Early American style hope chest.

The style of the large chest in Fig. 7-1 is Early American. The major structural pieces are mated with *splined miter* joints. Decorative trim is a distinctive feature of this chest. The wagon seat top is designed to hold a cushion. The large size (Fig. 7-2) makes the chest a dominant furniture piece.

CONSTRUCTION

Cut the front, back and end workpieces from birch plywood as specified in the *Bill of Material.* Rip the pieces to the specified width on the table saw. Tilt the saw blade to cut the miters. Use a long auxiliary board on the miter gauge to support the workpieces.

Cut the spline grooves in the edge miter. Use a ¼-inch dado head. Tilt the dado head to 45 degrees. Place the end being cut against the fence. Set the depth to ⅜ inch. Be sure the groove is correctly positioned, then cut it.

Cut the grooves for the bottom along the lower edges of the workpieces. Place them ¾ inch in from the edge and cut them ⅜ inch deep. Cut and fit the bottom piece. Cut the splines to fit. After performing a trial assembly, glue and clamp together the major pieces.

Machine the trim for the base of the chest. Shape it with a router in the router/shaper table. Use a ⅜ rounding over bit. Raise the bit to produce the square edge below the round. After shaping, cut the base trim to length, with 45-degree miters at the corners.

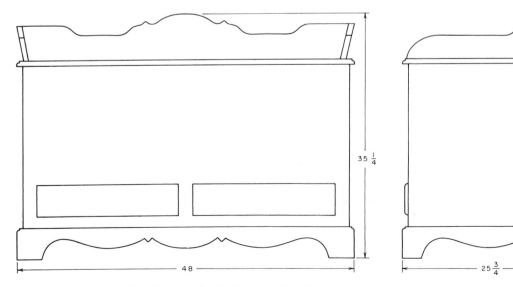

$35\frac{1}{4}$

48

$25\frac{3}{4}$

Fig. 7-2. Front and side views of the Early American hope chest.

BILL OF MATERIAL
Early American Hope Chest—Unit 7
(All dimensions are finished size)

Front and Back	2 pc. ¾″ x 23¾″ x 46½″	Birch Plywood
End	2 pc. ¾″ x 23¾″ x 24¼″	Birch Plywood
Bottom	1 pc. ¾″ x 23½″ x 45¾″	Fir Plywood
Splines	4 pc. ¼″ x ¾″ x 23¾″	Fir Plywood
Chest Upper-Edge Facing	2 pc. ½″ x ¾″ x 46½″	Maple
	2 pc. ½″ x ¾″ x 24¼″	Maple
Base Trim	2 pc. ¾″ x 4½″ x 48″	Maple
	2 pc. ¾″ x 4½″ x 25¾″	Maple
Drawer Fronts	2 pc. ½″ x 4½″ x 20¼″	Maple
Screws	4 pc. Flat Head, 1″, #8	
Handles	4 pc. Antique Brass	
Top	1 pc. ¾″ x 24¼″ x 46½″	Birch Plywood
Top Facing	1 pc. ¾″ x ¾″ x 48″	Maple
	2 pc. ¾″ x ¾″ x 25″	Maple
Top Trim	1 pc. ¾″ x 6¾″ x 48″	Maple
	2 pc. ¾″ x 5″ x 24″	Maple
Piano Hinge	1 pc. 1½″ x 48″	
Screws	15 pc. Flat Head, 1¼″, #8	
Plugs	4 pc. Oval Buttons	Maple

Enlarge the base trim patterns in Fig. 7-3 to finished size. Place the finished-size patterns on the base trim pieces for the sides and front. (The back base trim is not sculptured.) Trace around the patterns. Cut around the layout lines with the band saw, then sand the cuts. Glue the trim in place as shown in Fig. 7-4. Position the pieces 1½ inch from the bottom edge of the chest.

Cut the chest upper-edge facing to fit. Glue and attach it to the chest with brads (Fig. 7-5).

Cut the decorative drawer fronts. Shape their edges with a ¼ rounding over bit in the router/shaper table. Screw the drawer fronts to the chest fronts. Position them 1½ inch up from the base trim, with a 2-inch spacing on each side.

Cut the birch plywood top. Smooth the edges on the jointer. Cut the ¾ x ¾-inch top facing to fit, with miters at the front corners. Glue and clamp the facing to the top. With a hand-held router, shape the facing to match that on the base.

Machine the material for the top trim. Joint the bottom edges at a 10-degree angle. Enlarge the top-trim patterns in Fig. 7-6. Place

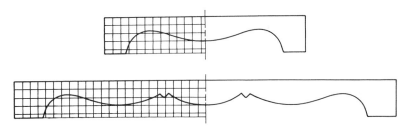

Fig. 7-3. Base trim patterns. The upper pattern is for the side base piece. The lower pattern is for the front base piece.

the correct pattern on the back side of each top-trim piece. Position the pattern flush with the bottom edge. Trace around the patterns.

Locate the correct positions for the compound miter joints. Cut the joints with the table saw. Set the blade at 45 degrees and the miter gauge at 10 degrees, either left or right. Make trial cuts on waste stock, to check the accuracy of the angles.

Cut the previously outlined decorative edges with the band saw. Tilt the table to 10 degrees. Cut from the lowest side of the blade. Sand the cuts either with the spindle sander or by hand. Be sure that the height of the back corners remains equal.

Position the top-trim pieces on the upper surface of the top. Space them ⅞ inch in from the side and back edges. Recheck the positioning and the squareness, then carefully mark their positions. Drill and attach each piece to the top surface with screws. Drill and install screws in the mitered joints. Plug the screw holes with buttons.

Fig. 7-4. Glue and clamp the base trim to the chest with parallel clamps.

Fig. 7-5. Partially completed chest, with ½-inch facing applied.

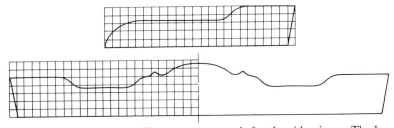

Fig. 7-6. Top trim patterns. The upper pattern is for the side pieces. The lower pattern is for the back piece.

FINISHING

Remove the decorative drawer fronts. Thoroughly sand the chest surfaces. Attach the top to the chest with a piano hinge. Apply Early American brown stain. Finish the surface with antique oil. Attach the handles to the drawer fronts, then reattach the fronts to the chest. Install commercial cedar lining in the chest interior, if desired. Position and install the lid-support mechanism and related hardware.

One-Drawer Nightstands

The design features and construction of two styles of nightstands are presented in this section. Both nightstands have one drawer and use the same basic two-shelf case design. The case is constructed with skeleton frames and veneered plywood ends and shelves. Dado and rabbet joints are used to mate the case pieces. The two distinct styles are created by using appropriate facing materials, trim and base shapes, decorative drawer fronts, and finishes.

Unit 8: Early American Nightstand

A sculptured base, solid-maple facing, and an ornate drawer pull establish the Early American style of this nightstand. Early American brown stain and antique oil create an appropriate surface finish.

Unit 9: Provincial Nightstand

Solid-oak facing and base materials, a slate formica top, and an unsculptured base give this nightstand a definite provincial appearance. Dark walnut stain and antique oil are used to emphasize the style.

33

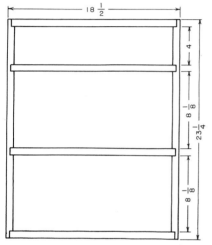

Fig. 8-1. Early American nightstand.

Unit 8
Early American Nightstand

The nightstand in Fig. 8-1 is designed to match existing Early American pieces. The sculptured frontpiece of the base, the shaped trim, and the use of maple facing establish the Early American style. The overall height (Fig. 8-2) also conforms to that of conventional Early American nightstands.

CASE CONSTRUCTION

Cut the ends of the case to the size specified in the *Bill of Material*. Smooth the edges on a jointer. Lay out the rabbet and dado joints for the shelves and skeleton frames (Fig. 8-3). Cut the grooves ⅜ inch deep with the dado head on the radial arm saw.

Fig. 8-3. Construction of the case.

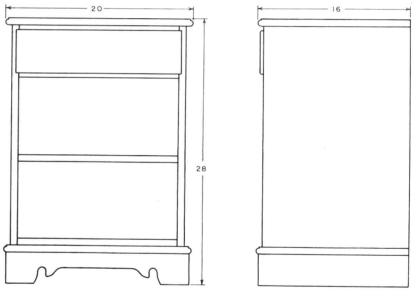

Fig. 8-2. Front and side views of the Early American nightstand.

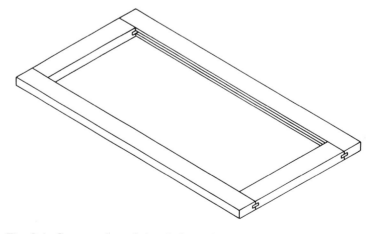

Fig. 8-4. Construction of the skeleton frames.

BILL OF MATERIAL
One-Drawer Nightstand—Unit 8
(All dimensions are finished size)

Case parts:

Ends	2 pc. ¾" x 15" x 23¼"	Birch Plywood
Shelf	2 pc. ¾" x 14¾" x 17¾"	Birch Plywood
Skeleton Frames	4 pc. ¾" x 1¾" x 17¾"	Poplar
	4 pc. ¾" x 1¾" x 11¾"	Poplar
Back	1 pc. ¼" x 17¾" x 23¼"	Birch Plywood
Facing	2 pc. ¼" x ¾" x 23¼"	Maple
	4 pc. ¼" x ¾" x 17"	Maple

Base Parts:

Apron	2 pc. ¾" x 2½" x 16"	Maple
	1 pc. ¾" x 2½" x 20"	Maple
Base	2 pc. ¾" x 3¼" x 15¾"	Maple
	1 pc. ¾" x 3¼" x 19½"	Maple
Cleats	2 pc. ¾" x ¾" x 13¼"	Poplar
	1 pc. ¾" x ¾" x 14½"	Poplar
Corner Blocks	2 pc. 1½" x 1½" x 3¼"	Poplar
Screws	21 pc. Flat Head, 1¼", #8	

Top Surface Parts:

Top	1 pc. ¾" x 15¼" x 18½"	Birch Plywood
Facing	2 pc. ¾" x ¾" x 16"	Maple
	1 pc. ¾" x ¾" x 20"	Maple
Screws	4 pc. Flat Head, 1¼", #10	

Drawer Parts:

Sides	2 pc. ½" x 3⅞" x 14½"	Pine
Front and Back	2 pc. ½" x 3⅞" x 16 7/16"	Pine
Bottom	1 pc. ¼" x 14" x 16 7/16"	Pine
Decorative Front	1 pc. ½" x 4½" x 17½"	Maple
Screws	2 pc. Flat Head, ¾", #8	
Drawer Pull	1 pc. Antique Brass	

Fig. 8-5. Hold the stiles upright in a fixture when cutting the grooves in their ends.

Fig. 8-6. Partially completed nightstand, with ¼-inch facing applied.

(This prevents chipping of the birch veneered surface.) Cuts will be made from both edges. Use the table saw to cut a ¼ x ⅜-inch rabbet on the back edges of the end pieces.

Cut the rails and the stiles for the skeleton frames (Fig. 8-4). Center a ¼ x ⅜-inch groove along one edge of each rail. Cut an identical groove in both ends of the stiles. Hold the stiles upright in a fixture when cutting the end grooves (Fig. 8-5). Glue and assemble the skeleton frames with splines. Clamp the frames and lay them on a flat surface until the glue sets.

Cut the two shelf pieces to finished size. Glue and assemble the case with bar clamps. Cut the piece for the back. Cut the ¼-inch facing for the case front. Attach the facing with glue and brads (Fig. 8-6).

Machine the material for the apron. Shape it with a router in the router/shaper table. Use a ⅜ rounding over bit. Raise the bit to create the square edge below the round. On the bottom edge, use only the round (Fig. 8-7).

Cut the apron pieces to fit, with mitered corners. The apron should extend out ¾ inch from the sides and the front of the case. Drill and attach the apron pieces to the case with glue and screws.

Machine the base material, then cut the base pieces to fit, with mitered corners. Enlarge the base pattern in Fig. 8-7. Place letters on the vertical grid lines in Fig. 8-7, and numbers on the horizontal lines. On a piece of heavy brown paper, rule a grid pattern of 1-inch squares. Letter and number the grid lines exactly as you did those in Fig. 8-7. Use these grid coordinates to transfer the pattern in Fig. 8-7 to the brown paper. Cut out the finished-size pattern. Place the finished-size pattern on the base front piece. Trace around the pattern, then cut around the layout lines with the band saw. Sand the cuts.

Assemble the base with corner blocks. Glue and clamp the miter joints with parallel clamps. Install cleats on the inner edges with glue and screws. Attach the base to the apron with screws. The base should be positioned ¼ inch in from the apron edges.

TOP CONSTRUCTION

Cut the birch plywood top. Smooth the edges on the jointer. Cut

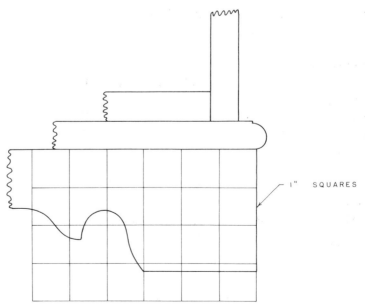

Fig. 8-7. Pattern for the base.

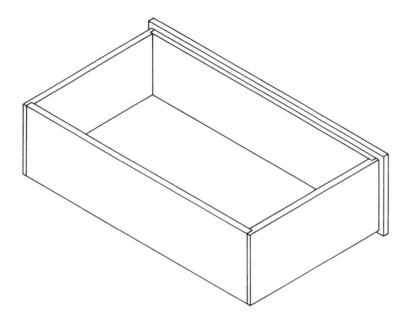

Fig. 8-8. Simple box construction is used for the drawers.

the top edge facing pieces, with miter joints at the corners. Edge glue the pieces to the top and then shape the edges the same as those on the apron. Slant drill through the uppermost skeleton frame. Attach the top to the skeleton frame with screws.

DRAWER CONSTRUCTION

Cut the front, back and side pieces for the drawer (Fig. 8-8). Make a ¼ x ¼-inch groove for the hardboard bottom in each piece. Position the grooves ¼ inch up from the lower edges of the pieces. Cut a ½-inch rabbet joint on the ends of the sides. Cut the joint ¼ inch deep. Cut and fit the bottom piece. Glue and assemble the drawer with finish nails.

Cut the decorative drawer front. Shape all of the edges with a ¼ rounding over bit. Correctly position the decorative front on the drawer front. The decorative front should overlap the drawer front by ¼ inch on the sides and bottom. Drill the drawer front and attach the decorative front to it with screws.

FINISHING

Thoroughly sand the cabinet surfaces. Apply Early American brown stain. Finish the surfaces with antique oil. Attach the drawer pull. Install the cabinet back with brads.

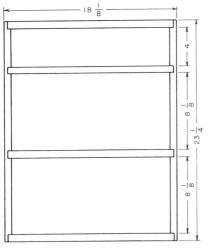

Fig. 9-1. Provincial style nightstand.

UNIT 9
Provincial Nightstand

The nightstand in Fig. 9-1 is designed to match provincial style furniture pieces. The base design, dark walnut finish, and shaped trim produce a distinctive provincial appearance. Slate formica is used on the top. The overall height (Fig. 9-2) conforms to that of conventional nightstands.

CASE CONSTRUCTION

Cut the end pieces of the case to size as indicated in the *Bill of Material*. Smooth the edges on the jointer. Lay out on the end pieces the rabbet and dado joints for the shelves and the skeleton frames (Fig. 9-3). Cut the grooves ⅜-inch deep with a dado head on the radial arm saw. This eliminates chipping of the birch veneered surfaces. Cuts will be made from both edges. Use the table saw to cut the ¼ x ⅜-inch rabbet on the back edges of the end pieces.

Cut the rails and stiles for the skeleton frames (Fig. 9-4). Center and cut a ¼ x ⅜-inch groove along one edge of each rail. Cut an identical groove on both ends of the stiles. Hold the stiles upright in a fixture when making the cuts (Fig. 9-5). Cut the splines, then glue and assemble the skeleton frame. Clamp the assembly until the glue dries.

Cut the shelves to size. Then, glue and assemble the case with bar clamps. Cut the back material and the ¼-inch facing for the

Fig. 9-3. Construction of the case.

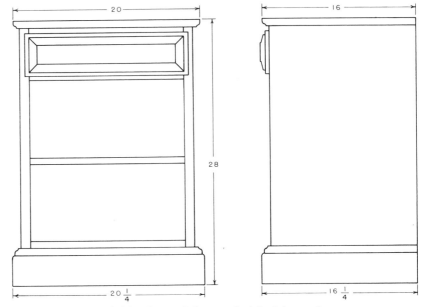

Fig. 9-2. Front and side views of the provincial nightstand.

BILL OF MATERIAL
One-Drawer Nightstand—Unit 9
(All dimensions are finished size)

Case Parts:

Ends	2 pc. ¾″ x 15″ x 23¼″	Birch Plywood
Shelf	2 pc. ¾″ x 14¾″ x 17¾″	Birch Plywood
Skeleton Frames	4 pc. ¾″ x 1¾″ x 17¾″	Poplar
	4 pc. ¾″ x 1¾″ x 11¾″	Poplar
Back	1 pc. ¼″ x 17¾″ x 23¼″	Birch Plywood
Facing	2 pc. ¼″ x 1″ x 23¼″	Oak
	4 pc. ¼″ x ¾″ x 16½″	Oak

Base Parts:

Apron	2 pc. ¾″ x 2½″ x 16″	Oak
	1 pc. ¾″ x 2½″ x 20″	Oak
Base	2 pc. ¾″ x 3¼″ x 16¼″	Oak
	1 pc. ¾″ x 3¼″ x 20½″	Oak
Cleats	2 pc. ¾″ x ¾″ x 14″	Poplar
	1 pc. ¾″ x ¾″ x 15″	Poplar
Corner Blocks	2 pc. 1½″ x 1½″ x 3¼″	Poplar
Screws	21 pc. Flat Head, 1¼″, #8	

Top Surface Parts:

Top	1 pc. ¾″ x 15¼″ x 18½″	Fir Plywood
Facing	2 pc. ¾″ x ¾″ x 16″	Oak
	1 pc. ¾″ x ¾″ x 20″	Oak
Formica	1 pc. 16¼″ x 20¼″	Slate
Screws	4 pc. Flat Head, 1¼″, #10	

Drawer Parts:

Sides	2 pc. ½″ x 3⅞″ x 14½″	Pine
Front and Back	2 pc. ½″ x 3⅞″ x 15⅞″	Pine
Bottom	1 pc. ¼″ x 14½″ x 15⅜″	Hardboard
Decorative Front	1 pc. ½″ x 4½″ x 17½″	Oak
Secondary Front	1 pc. ½″ x 3¼″ x 16¼″	Oak
Side Guides	2 pc. ¼″ x ¾″ x 14½″	Pine
Screws	4 pc. Flat Head, ¾″, #8	
Drawer Pull	1 pc. Provincial	

Fig. 9-5. The stiles should be held upright in a fixture when grooves are being cut in their ends.

Fig. 9-6. Partially completed night-stand, with ¼-inch facing applied to the case front.

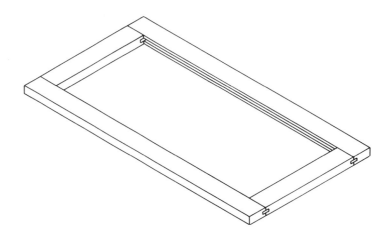

Fig. 9-4. Construction of the skeleton frames

case front. Attach the facing to the case front with glue and brads (Fig. 9-6).

Machine the material for the apron. Place a router in the router/shaper table. Use a 3/16 *ogee* bit to shape the apron material as shown in Fig. 9-7. Cut the apron pieces to fit, with mitered corners. The apron should extend out ¾ inch from the sides and the front of the cabinet. Drill and attach the apron to the case with glue and screws.

BASE CONSTRUCTION

Cut the base pieces to fit, with mitered corners. The base should be set out ¼ inch from the apron. Shape the base pieces with a ⅜ rounding over bit in the router/shaper table (Fig. 9-7).

Cut the corner blocks. Glue and assemble the base pieces. Clamp the miter joints with parallel clamps. Install cleats on the inner edges with glue and screws. Attach the base to the apron with screws.

TOP CONSTRUCTION

Cut the fir plywood *top*. Smooth the edges on the jointer. Cut

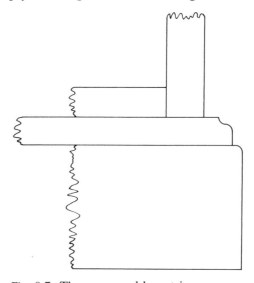

Fig. 9-7. The apron and base trim.

the facing to fit, with miter joints at the corners. Edge glue the facing to the top, then shape the edges the same as those on the apron.

Cut the slate formica and apply it to the top piece with contact cement. Trim the edges with a carbide-tipped formica bit in the router. Slant drill holes through the top skeleton frame. Attach the top to the skeleton frame with screws.

DRAWER CONSTRUCTION

Cut the material for the drawer (Fig. 9-8). Cut a ¼ x ¼-inch groove for the hardboard bottom. Place the groove ¼ inch up from the bottom edge of the front, back and side pieces. Cut ½-inch rabbet joints on the ends of the sides. Cut the rabbets ¼ inch deep. Cut and fit the bottom piece. Glue and assemble the drawer pieces with finish nails.

Cut the material for the decorative drawer front. Position the decorative front so that there is a ½-inch overlap between its edges and the sides and top of the front piece. Drill the front piece and attach the decorative front with screws.

Prepare to cut the secondary drawer front. Tilt the table saw blade to 10 degrees and raise it to ⅞ inch. Set the fence and rip a bevel on all edges of the workpiece. Prepare to make a second cut with the workpiece flat. Set the blade at a right-angle to the workpiece surface and raise it to ⅛ inch. Set the fence and rip the edges (Fig. 9-8). Crosscut the ends with the aid of a miter gauge. Sand the workpiece to eliminate saw marks. Center the secondary front on the decorative front. Drill holes and attach the secondary front to the decorative front. Glue the drawer side guides into the cabinet.

FINISHING

Thoroughly sand the cabinet surfaces. Apply dark walnut stain. Finish with antique oil. Attach the drawer pull, and install the back piece with brads.

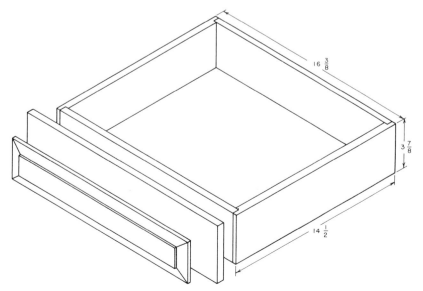

Fig. 9-8. Construction of the drawer.

Utility Cabinets

The design features and construction of three types of utility cabinets are described in this section. Each cabinet is designed for a specific purpose, and each emphasizes one or more special construction features.

Unit 10: Entertainment Center
This open-type cabinet provides shelf space for stereo components, speakers and records. The simple styling makes it suitable for most decors. Knock-down construction permits easy disassembly and reassembly. Specific construction features include tapered legs and birch dowel uprights with rosan inserts and hanger bolts.

Unit 11: Wall Shelf
This cabinet is designed for displaying and storing art objects and other collectables. Construction features include a veneered back panel, recessed shelves and drawers, and solid-cherry case pieces mated by box joints.

Unit 12: Bathroom Cabinet
Designed for storage of towels and other bathroom articles, this cabinet features sliding doors, a vinyl-covered top, and enameled surfaces. Major case pieces are of easily painted birch plywood and poplar facing. The hardboard doors slide easily on plastic tracks.

43

Fig. 10-1. Entertainment center of knock-down construction.

UNIT 10
Entertainment Center

The style of the entertainment center in Fig. 10-1 makes it suitable for any setting. The design provides appropriate shelf spaces for stereo components, speakers and records. The overall dimensions are shown in Fig. 10-2. The shelves are birch plywood with solid wood facing. The knock-down construction (Fig. 10-3) makes transporting easy.

CONSTRUCTION

Cut the birch plywood surfaces to the sizes indicated in the *Bill of Material*. Rip the material with the table saw and perform crosscuts with the radial arm saw. Be sure the good side of the material is up when cutting. Smooth all edges with the jointer.

Select the material for the solid-maple facing. Joint all adjacent edges to develop registration surfaces. Plane the large facing pieces to the exact thickness of the plywood. (The finished size of sanded ¾-inch plywood is usually slightly less than ¾ inch.) Rip the facing to the required width, with allowance for planing both surfaces. Plane the facing to a thickness of ½ inch.

Cut the facing pieces to the required lengths, with 45-degree miters on the ends. Fit each piece to its corresponding shelf surface. Edge glue and attach the facing to the shelf surfaces with bar clamps. Wash off any excess glue. After the glue dries, sand all facing flush with the veneered surfaces of the shelves.

Machine the material for the tapered legs. Prepare it for spindle turning and then taper the diameter of each leg from 1 inch to 1¾ inch. Cut the legs to 3-inch lengths. Cut the 1-inch dowel material for the uprights to the required lengths.

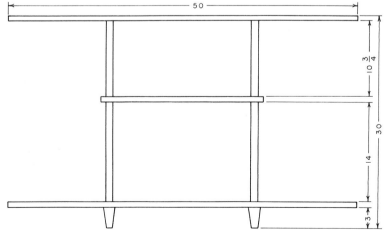

Fig. 10-2. Front view of entertainment center.

BILL OF MATERIAL
Entertainment Center—Unit 10
(All dimensions are finished size)

Shelves	2 pc. ¾″ x 15″ x 49″	Birch Plywood
	1 pc. ¾″ x 15″ x 22″	Birch Plywood
Facing	4 pc. ½″ x ¾″ x 50″	Maple
	6 pc. ½″ x ¾″ x 16″	Maple
	2 pc. ½″ x ¾″ x 23″	Maple
Uprights	4 pc. 1″ dia. x 14″	Birch Dowel
	4 pc. 1″ dia. x 10 ¾″	Birch Dowel
Legs	4 pc. 2″ x 2″ x 3½″	Maple
Rosan Inserts	12 pc. ¼″	
Hanger Bolts	4 pc. ¼″ x 2″	
	8 pc. ¼″ x 2½″	

Fig. 10-3. Finished parts ready for assembly. No tools are required for assembly or disassembly.

Drill ¼-inch-diameter holes in the corners of the *center* shelf. Position the holes 1¼ inch in from the sides and 1¾ inch in from the front and back edges.

Drill ¼-inch-diameter holes in the *lower* shelf. Use the drilled center shelf as a guide to correctly position the holes in the lower shelf. Position the center shelf 13½ inches in from the side of the lower shelf. Mark the hole positions, remove the center shelf, then drill the holes in the lower shelf.

Prepare to drill a ⅜-inch-diameter hole in one end of all uprights. Locate the center of each upright with the centering head of a combination square. Hold the pieces upright in a drill-press vise when drilling.

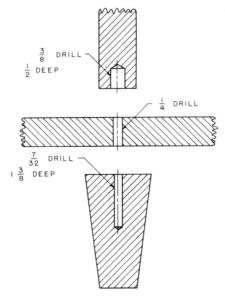

Fig. 10-4. Details of the method by which the legs and uprights are attached to the shelves.

45

Copyright © 1979 by The Bobbs-Merrill Company, Inc.

Mark and drill ⅜-inch-diameter holes in the top shelf. Use the center shelf as a guide. Position it as described for drilling the lower shelf. Drill the holes ½ inch deep. Install the rosan inserts with a large screwdriver.

Drill a 7/32-inch-diameter hole in the legs and in the undrilled upright ends (Fig. 10-4). Insert the 2½-inch hanger bolts in the legs and long uprights. Allow them to protrude 1⅛ inch. Insert the 2-inch hanger bolts in the short uprights. Allow them to protrude ⅜ inch. The hanger bolts are easily installed with two nuts locked against each other.

ASSEMBLY AND FINISHING

Assemble the unit upside down. Screw the short uprights into the top piece. Position the center shelf and screw in the long uprights. Position the lower shelf and screw in the legs.

Disassemble the parts and thoroughly sand all of them. Apply Early American brown stain and finish with antique oil. When the finish is completely dried, reassemble the pieces.

UNIT 11
Wall Shelf

The wall shelf shown in Figs. 11-1 and 11-2 is specifically designed to display art objects and other collectables. The various sizes of open areas are designed to frame the displayed objects. The shelves and drawers are recessed to create a shadow effect. The hole-type drawer pulls add to this effect (Fig. 11-3). A natural oil finish is used to accent the grain.

CONSTRUCTION

Select the material for the major cabinet pieces as specified in the *Bill of Material*. Prepare registration surfaces on all pieces. Match the grain, then edge glue the 10-inch-wide pieces. Plane all pieces to a 5/8-inch thickness. Cut the prepared pieces to the widths and lengths required for the sides, top and bottom, partition and shelves.

Cut the rails and stiles for the skeleton frames (Fig. 11-4). Center a ¼ x ⅜-inch groove on one edge of each rail. Cut an identical groove in both ends of the stiles while holding the pieces upright in a fixture (Fig. 11-5). Perform a trial assembly, then glue the pieces, assemble with splines, and clamp the assembly.

Prepare to cut the box joints on the ends of the top, bottom and side pieces (Fig. 11-6). Cut these joints with a dado head on the table saw. First, attach an auxiliary board with a step block to the miter gauge. Cut a 1¼-inch notch in the auxiliary board. Next, move the auxiliary board 1¼ inch to the right and screw it to the miter gauge. Place a notched step block in the opening. The first step locates the right of the cut. A ⅝-inch-thick shim should be used to move the workpiece forward as required. The second step

Fig. 11-1. Wall shelf for display/storage of collectables.

Fig. 11-3. Recessed shelves and drawers and hole-type drawer pulls create a shadow effect.

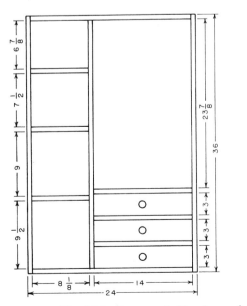

Fig. 11-2. Front and side views of the wall shelf.

Fig 11-5. Hold the stiles upright in a fixture when cutting the grooves in their ends.

Fig. 11-6. Box joints are used to mate the ends of the top, bottom and side pieces.

BILL OF MATERIAL
Wall Shelf—Unit 11
(All dimensions are finished size)

Cabinet Parts:

Sides	2 pc.	$\frac{5}{8}''$ x 10" x 36"	Cherry
Top and Bottom	2 pc.	$\frac{5}{8}''$ x 10" x 24"	Cherry
Partition	1 pc.	$\frac{5}{8}''$ x $9\frac{5}{8}''$ x $35\frac{1}{4}''$	Cherry
Shelf	3 pc.	$\frac{5}{8}''$ x $9\frac{1}{8}''$ x $8\frac{5}{8}''$	Cherry
	1 pc.	$\frac{5}{8}''$ x $9\frac{5}{8}''$ x $14\frac{1}{2}''$	Cherry
Skeleton Frames	4 pc.	$\frac{5}{8}''$ x 2" x $14\frac{1}{2}''$	Cherry
	4 pc.	$\frac{5}{8}''$ x 2" x $5\frac{5}{8}''$	Cherry
Splines	8 pc.	$\frac{1}{4}''$ x $\frac{1}{2}''$ x 2"	Fir Plywood
Back	1 pc.	$\frac{1}{4}''$ x $23\frac{1}{4}''$ x $35\frac{1}{4}''$	Hardboard
	2 pc.	$23\frac{1}{4}''$ x $35\frac{1}{4}''$	Cherry Veneer

Drawer Parts:

Front	3 pc.	$\frac{5}{8}''$ x 3" x 14"	Cherry
Back	3 pc.	$\frac{1}{2}''$ x 3" x $13\frac{1}{2}''$	Poplar
Sides	6 pc.	$\frac{1}{2}''$ x 3" x $8\frac{3}{4}''$	Poplar
Bottom	3 pc.	$\frac{1}{8}''$ x $8\frac{1}{4}''$ x $13\frac{1}{2}''$	Hardboard

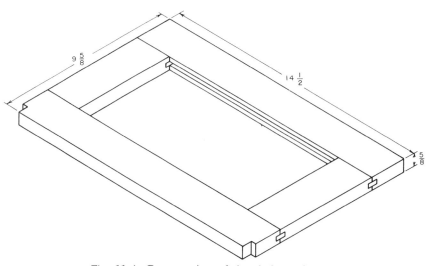

Fig. 11-4. Construction of the skeleton frames.

locates the left of the cut. Practice and adjustments are necessary to develop the required accuracy.

Cut $\frac{1}{4}$-inch-deep *stop dados* for the partition, the shelves and the skeleton frames. Cut these joints on the radial arm saw, to avoid chipping. The dado joints in the right section of the cabinet should permit the pieces to fit flush with the front. The dado joints in the left section should permit the shelves to set back $\frac{1}{2}$ inch from the front. Notch the shelves and skeleton frames to fit the dado joints. The back panel is placed in a $\frac{1}{4}$ x $\frac{3}{8}$-inch rabbet. Cut the rabbet all the way through on the table saw. Plug the box joints where the rabbet shows.

VENEERED PANEL FABRICATION

Select the cherry veneer for the back panel. To assure a stable workpiece, veneer both the face and the back surface of the hardboard. The hardboard and the veneer material should be cut over-size and trimmed later to finish size.

Clamp the veneer between plywood (Fig. 11-7) and joint the edges. Tape the veneer splices and splits with brown paper tape. (Do *not* use masking tape. Pressure would force the tape into the wood pores.) For easy removal later, place the tape on the *outside* surfaces of the veneer.

Attach the veneer to the hardboard front and back surfaces with plastic resin glue. If a means of applying pressure is not available, use contact cement.

Fig. 11-7. Clamp the veneer between plywood pieces when jointing it.

The correct mixture of plastic resin glue and water depends on the number of square feet to be covered. Use 12.5 grams of glue and 7.5 grams of water per square foot. In this case there are four 5.7 square-foot surfaces, producing a total of 22.8 square feet to be covered. The correct amount of glue therefore is (22.8 x 12.5 grams), or 285 grams. The correct amount of water is (22.8 x 7.5 grams), or 171 grams.

Mix the water with the glue a little at a time. When thoroughly mixed, brush the mixture on the hardboard surfaces and on the *back* surfaces of the veneer. Apply enough mixture to make the surfaces appear well wetted. Position the veneer on the hardboard and apply pressure. Allow sufficient drying time. After drying is complete, trim the veneered panel to finished size. Carefully scrape off the tape and sand the surfaces.

CABINET ASSEMBLY

Perform a trial assembly of the cabinet box. If the pieces all fit correctly, glue and reassemble them. Use pressure blocks and bar clamps. The top, bottom and sides may be glued and assembled first, and the partition and shelves later inserted from the back. Wash off any excess glue.

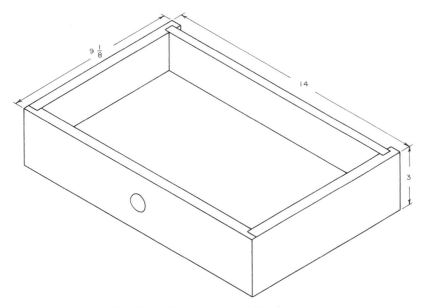

Fig. 11-8. Construction of the drawers.

Fig. 11-9. Finished drawers installed in the wall shelf. Note the flush construction.

DRAWER CONSTRUCTION

Cut the material for the drawers (Fig. 11-8). Cut a $\frac{1}{8}$ x $\frac{1}{4}$-inch groove for the hardboard bottom $\frac{1}{4}$ inch up from the edge of all pieces. Cut $\frac{1}{2}$-inch rabbet joints on the ends of the front. Cut the rabbets 5/16 inch deep. Cut $\frac{1}{2}$-inch dado joints on the drawer sides. Cut these joints $\frac{1}{4}$ inch in from the back edge and $\frac{1}{4}$ inch deep. Cut and fit the bottom piece. Drill a 1-inch-diameter hole for the pull in each drawer front. Drill the holes at a 30-degree angle. Glue and assemble the drawers with finish nails (Fig. 11-9).

FINISHING

Thoroughly sand the cabinet surfaces and back. Sand off all sharp corners. Finish the surfaces with Danish oil. After the finish has dried, attach the back panel to the cabinet with brads.

UNIT 12
Bathroom Cabinet

Fig. 12-1. Bathroom cabinet equipped with sliding doors.

The bathroom cabinet in Fig. 12-1 provides storage space for towels and personal items. Sliding doors permit easy access in confined quarters. The cabinet is made of birch plywood, which provides a good surface for painting. The plastic top material is easily cut with hand tools.

CONSTRUCTION

Begin construction by fabricating the basic case (Fig. 12-2). Cut the ends, shelves and toeboard from birch plywood as specified in the *Bill of Material*. Rip the pieces to width on the table saw. Crosscut to length on the radial arm saw, to avoid chipping. Smooth all of the edges with the jointer.

Layout dado joints on the end pieces. Cut the ⅜ x ¾-inch dado joints with a dado head on the radial arm saw. Note that the joints for the middle shelf should stop 1 inch from the edge.

Layout the dado joints on the top. The joints should stop ¾ inch from the edge. Position the joints so that the top overhangs the case ¾ inch on all sides. Square out all of the stop dado joints with a chisel.

Fig. 12-3. Closeup showing the details of the toeboard, facing and the sliding door track.

Cut a ¼ x ⅜-inch rabbet on the end pieces. Use a dado head on the table saw. Position matching grooves in the top. Cut the grooves all the way through the ends of the top. Carry out a trial assembly of the case. If the pieces fit correctly, glue and assemble the case with finish nails.

Cut the toeboard and attach it to the case with glue and finish nails (Fig. 12-3). Cut the plastic slide material to the specified

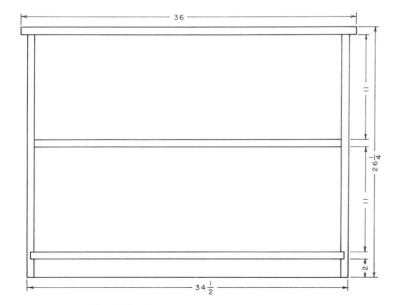

Fig. 12-2. Front view of case construction.

51

BILL OF MATERIAL
Bathroom Cabinet—Unit 12
(All dimensions are finished size)

Top	1 pc. ¾″ x 12″ x 36″	Fir Plywood
Ends	2 pc. ¾″ x 10¼″ x 25⅞″	Birch Plywood
Middle Shelf	1 pc. ¾″ x 9″ x 33¾″	Birch Plywood
Bottom Shelf	1 pc. ¾″ x 10″ x 33¾″	Birch Plywood
Toeboard	1 pc. ¾″ x 2″ x 33″	Birch Plywood
Facing	2 pc. ¼″ x 1″ x 25½″	Poplar
	1 pc. ¼″ x 1″ x 32½″	Poplar
	1 pc. ¼″ x ¾″ x 33″	Poplar
	1 pc. ¼″ x ½″ x 32½″	Poplar
Back	1 pc. ¼″ x 23⅞″ x 33¾″	Hardboard
Doors	2 pc. ¼″ x 17⅛″ x 22⅜″	Hardboard
Top Material	1 pc. 12¼″ x 36¼″	Plastic
	2 pc. 1″ x 12¼″	Plastic
	2 pc. 1″ x 36¼″	Plastic
Plastic Track	2 pc. ½″ x 1″ x 33″	Plastic

length. Install a deeply grooved piece on the top to permit door removal.

Machine the facing material from poplar. Install the 1-inch vertical pieces on the ends with glue and brads. Be sure the overlap is on the inside so that it will cover the edges of the doors. Install a 1-inch facing piece at the bottom to cover the plastic slide. Drill the edge of the ½-inch trim piece and install it at the top to cover the plastic slide. Glue and nail the ¾-inch center facing.

Cut the doors and the back from hardboard that is smooth on two sides. Drill the holes for the pulls. Position the holes 2 inches in and 6 inches down from the top.

Cut the plastic material for the top with large scissors or tin snips. Install it with contact cement. Attach the end pieces and trim with a matte knife, hand plane or file. Attach the front and back pieces. Attach the completed top to the case. To assure good contact, tap with a block of wood and a mallet.

FINISHING

Set all nails with a nail set and fill the holes. Thoroughly sand the cabinet and doors. Apply enamel undercoat and finish with two coats of white enamel paint. Install the back with brads, and insert the doors in the tracks.

Coffee Tables

The design features and construction of four styles of coffee tables are described in this section. The design of any of the four styles can be altered to suit the individual taste of the student. The dimensions also can be altered to construct companion end tables or to match existing companion pieces.

Unit 13: Modern Coffee Table
The bold, straight-line design of this table is highlighted by decorative spline joints. The specified dimensions produce a shape which is slightly wider and lower than traditional coffee tables.

Unit 14: Contemporary Coffee Table
Straight, simple lines, walnut stock, and the absence of decorative trim give this table an unmistakable contemporary look. The principle structural pieces are mated by mortise/tenon joints.

Unit 15: Trestle Coffee Table
The distinctively informal appearance of this style is established by a plain top and smoothly sculptured legs supported by a crossmember with pinned mortise/tenon joints. The use of antiqued pine enhances the warm, casual look of this table.

Unit 16: Early American Coffee Table
Turned, ornamental legs and antiqued pine give this table a distinctively Early American style. The base structure is mated with mortise/tenon joints.

UNIT 13
Modern Coffee Table

The modern-style coffee table in Fig. 13-1 features a bold, straight-line design. This table is slightly wider and lower than traditional coffee tables (Fig. 13-2). The structure emphasizes the decorative spline joint.

CONSTRUCTION

Begin construction by selecting and cutting the pieces for the legs and base as specified in the *Bill of Material*. Cut the maple pieces to rough size. Joint the adjacent edges to develop registration surfaces. Use the planer to assure uniform thickness and width. Cut the maple pieces to length, with the appropriate angles on the ends.

Install a ½-inch dado head in the table saw. Prepare to cut the grooves for the splines. Secure the leg in a fixture like that in Fig. 13-3. Attach the fixture to the miter gauge. Position the spline grooves ⅜ inch from the inside corner of the miter. Cut the grooves ½ inch deep.

Select the material for the splines and plane the board to the required thickness. Cut 1-inch splines from the material, with the grain perpendicular (90 degrees) to the long edge. Temporarily

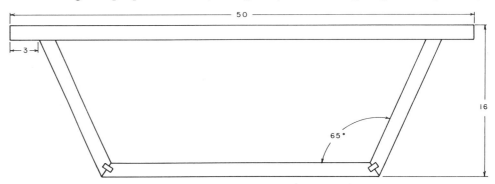

Fig. 13-2. Front view of the modern coffee table.

Fig. 13-3. Fixture for securing the leg members during cutting of the spline grooves.

Fig. 13-4. The recommended method of clamping the splined miter leg joints.

BILL OF MATERIAL
Modern Coffee Table—Unit 13
(All dimensions are finished size)

Top	1 pc. ¾″ x 23¼″ x 49¼″	Birch Plywood	
Facing	2 pc. ¾″ x 1½″ x 50″	Maple	
	2 pc. ¾″ x 1½″ x 24″	Maple	
Legs	4 pc. 1½″ x 1¾″ x 16½″	Maple	
Base	2 pc. 1½″ x 1¾″ x 29¾″	Maple	
Spline Material	1 pc. ½″ x 2″ x 10″	Walnut	
	1 pc. ¼″ x 1¾″ x 10″	Walnut	
Dowel Pins	4 pc. ⅜″ x 1½″	Birch	

Fig. 13-5. Finished leg joint after the spline of the splined miter joint has been sanded flush.

Fig. 13-6. Finished top facing splined miter joint after the spline has been sanded flush.

assemble the leg members to check the fit of the joints. The splines will protrude from the sides of the joints. The protrusions should be sanded flush after permanent assembly of the leg members.

Glue and clamp the leg members (Fig. 13-4). Small parallel clamps should be tightly secured to the leg members. Pressure then should be applied to the joints with larger clamps.

Select and cut the birch plywood piece for the top surface. Joint and plane the facing material to finished size. Center a ⅜-inch-deep groove on the inner surface of all facing pieces. Cut the facing to length, with 45-degree angles on the ends.

Cut the grooves for the top facing splines in the edge miter. Use a ¼-inch dado head and tilt it to 45 degrees. Place the end being cut against the fence and correctly position the groove. After setting the depth to ⅜ inch, advance the workpiece with the miter gauge. Back up all pieces with an auxiliary board.

Select the material for the top facing splines. Plane the board to the desired thickness. Cut ¾-inch splines from the material, with the grain perpendicular to the long edge. Temporarily assemble the facing around the top to check the fit of the joints. Glue and clamp the facing joints with bar clamps. Do *not* glue the facing to the top panel; instead, allow it to 'float'.

Drill ⅜-inch dowel holes in the legs. Position the leg assembly 2 inches from the top edges and 3 inches from the ends. Mark matching holes in the bottom surface of the top with dowel centers. Drill the ⅜-inch dowel holes. Glue and clamp the leg assembly to the top with bar clamps.

FINISHING

Carry out final sanding of all surfaces. Sand the splines flush (Figs. 13-5 and 13-6). Eliminate all sharp corners. Finish the surfaces with Danish oil.

Fig. 14-1. Contemporary coffee table.

UNIT 14
Contemporary Coffee Table

The contemporary coffee table in Fig. 14-1 has been designed with simplicity and informality in mind. This is achieved through the use of straight-line design and an absence of additional decoration. The relatively small size (Fig. 14-2) makes the table suitable for a variety of uses.

TOP AND SHELF MATERIAL SELECTION

Selection and fabrication of the material for the top and shelf provides an opportunity to make interesting use of sapwood. As is evident in Fig. 14-3, the grain and coloration of this wood can be used to create a very pleasing striped effect. To produce this effect, select and match the grains and widths of available rough boards.

The top and shelf surfaces are fabricated from open-grain walnut stock as specified in the *Bill of Material*. Select the pieces and mate them with glued, edge-to-edge butt joints.

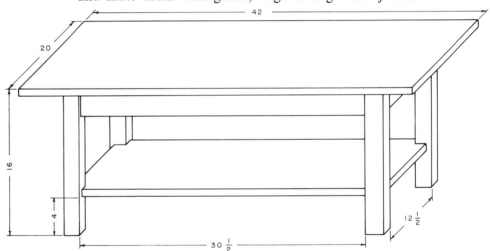

Fig. 14-2. Three-dimensional view of the contemporary coffee table.

Fig. 14-3. The distinctive grain and coloration of sapwood give the top and shelf a pleasing striped effect.

Fig. 14-4. The major structural pieces are mated with mortise/tenon joints. The rails are recessed ¼ inch from the outer surfaces of the legs.

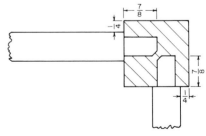

Fig. 14-5. Correct layout of the blind mortise/tenon joints which mate the legs and rails.

56

BILL OF MATERIAL
Contemporary Coffee Table—Unit 14
(All dimensions are finished size)

Top	1 pc. ¾″ x 20″ x 42″	Walnut
Shelf	1 pc. ¾″ x 15″ x 33″	Walnut
Legs	4 pc. 1¾″ x 1¾″ x 15¼″	Walnut
Rails	2 pc. ¾″ x 3″ x 32¼″	Walnut
	2 pc. ¾″ x 3″ x 14¼″	Walnut
Cleats	2 pc. ¾″ x ¾″ x 28½″	Poplar
	2 pc. ¾″ x ¾″ x 12″	Poplar
Screws	28 pc. Flat Head, 1¼″, #8	

CONSTRUCTION

The basic structure (Fig. 14-4) is joined with mortise and tenon joints between the legs and rails. The blind mortise and tenon (Fig. 14-5) is ½ x 2 inches and centered on the ¾ x 3-inch rails. The rails are inset ¼ inch from the face of the legs. The lower shelf is held in place by notching the legs (Fig. 14-6). The notch is cut with a dado head on the table saw. Secure the leg in a V-block during the crosscutting operation. All joints in the legs should be cut first, and corresponding parts fitted to these. Notches cut in the shelf corners hold the shelf in place between the legs (Figs. 14-7 and 14-8). This produces a very clean appearance at the corners. The top is held in place by ¾-inch-square cleats with screws.

FINISHING

Prepare for finishing by filling all knots with dark stick shellac. This enhances the natural appearance. Thoroughly sand all exposed surfaces. During sanding, slightly round all corners, to eliminate sharpness. Apply several coats of oil finish, and sand with silicon carbide paper while wet.

Fig. 14-6. Correct layout of the mortises and notches in the legs.

Fig. 14-7. The layout of the notches which hold the shelf in place between the legs.

Fig. 14-8. Carefully notched legs and shelf corners produce a clean appearance.

UNIT 15
Trestle Coffee Table

Fig. 15-1. Trestle-style coffee table.

The trestle coffee table in Fig. 15-1 presents a very sturdy, informal impression. The antiqued pine produces a warm appearance. The plain top and leg shape (Fig. 15-2) add to the informality. The table is particularly suitable for casual settings.

CONSTRUCTION

Begin construction by selecting pieces for the legs (Fig. 15-3). Prepare to edge glue the pieces together, with the joint at the center. Cut the 1 x 2-inch mortise with the table saw before gluing the pieces together. Cut the mortise ½ inch deep on the edge of each piece. Position the mortise 7 inches from the bottom end. Align the mortise cuts, and glue and clamp the pieces.

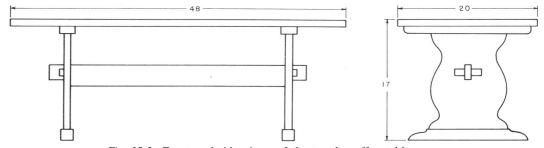

Fig. 15-2. Front and side views of the trestle coffee table.

Prepare to enlarge the leg pattern in Fig. 15-4. Rule 1-inch squares on a large piece of wrapping paper. Letter the vertical lines and number the horizontal lines of the pattern in Fig. 15-4. Place corresponding letters and numbers on the full-size pattern grid. Locate specific points on the pattern in Fig. 15-4 and transfer them to the full-size pattern grid. Use a thin, flexible piece of wood to connect the points. Cut out the pattern and place it on the leg

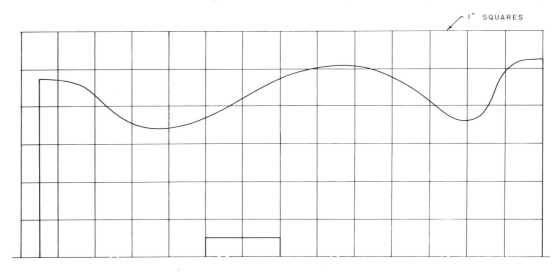

Fig. 15-4. The pattern for the legs.

BILL OF MATERIAL
Trestle Coffee Table—Unit 15
(All dimensions are finished size)

Top	1 pc. 1″ x 20″ x 48″	Pine
Legs	2 pc. 1″ x 10½″ x 13½″	Pine
Foot	2 pc. 1½″ x 1¾″ x 17″	Pine
Leg Top	2 pc. 1″ x 2¼″ x 18″	Pine
Cross		
Member	1 pc. 1″ x 3″ x 37″	Pine
Pin	2 pc. ⅝″ x 1″ x 4″	Pine
Screws	12 pc. Flat Head, 1½″, #8	
	6 pc. Flat Head, 2″, #10	
Dowel Pins	6 pc. ⅜″ x 2½″	Birch

Fig. 15-3. Each leg of the table is fabricated from two pieces of pine. The pieces are edge glued together after the mortise is cut.

Fig. 15-6. A ⅜-inch shoulder exists around the base of each foot.

pieces. Trace the pattern on the workpieces, then band saw and sand the legs to the outlined shape.

Select and glue together the material for the feet. Make a full-size enlargement of the foot pattern in Fig. 15-5. Cut out the pattern and place it on the foot pieces. Trace around the pattern, then band saw and sand the foot pieces to produce the required shape.

Drill three evenly spaced dowel holes in the bottom ends of the legs. Use a self-centering dowel-it jig. Drill the dowel holes 1½ inch deep. Correctly position and drill matching holes in the feet. Trial fit the workpieces, then glue them together. Clamp the joints with bar clamps. The relative sizes of the leg and foot workpieces assure a ⅜-inch shoulder around the base of the feet (Fig. 15-6).

Cut the leg top pieces with a ½-inch-radius curve on the ends. Center the pieces on the top of the legs. Drill and countersink holes for the three 2-inch screws in each leg top piece. Space the screw holes evenly. Drill and countersink holes in the inner edge of each top piece for the three 1½ inch screws. Attach the leg tops to the legs, then sand the leg assembly. Sand down all edges to produce a worn appearance.

Cut the cross member to the specified size. To produce the tenon, lay out and cut 1 x 3-inch notches in the lower edge of each end (Fig. 15-7). Fit the tenon to the leg mortise. Slight filing of the mortise might be needed. Cut the mortise for the pin in the cross member. Space and size the mortise so that the pin tightens the base assembly.

Select the pieces for the top, and edge glue them together. Cut and plane the joined pieces to the specified size. Sand the ends with a belt sander. Additional boards may be clamped on each side to

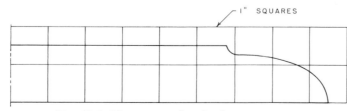

Fig. 15-5. The pattern for the feet.

59

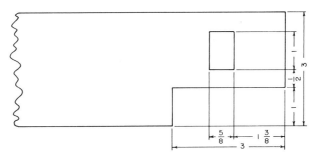

Fig. 15-7. The layout of the tenon at each end of the cross member.

assure squareness. Sand down the corners to produce a worn look. Center the top on the base assembly, then position and drill the screw holes.

FINISHING

Disassemble the pieces and perform final sanding. Apply dark walnut stain to the pieces and reassemble them. Spray on several ·coats of lacquer sealer. Sand between coats. For a final finish, apply two coats of dull-rubbed finishing lacquer.

UNIT 16
Early American Coffee Table

The Early American coffee table in Fig. 16-1 has a casual look. The antiqued pine produces a warm appearance. The turned legs add a degree of elegance. The table size (Fig. 16-2) makes it particularly suitable for smaller family rooms.

CONSTRUCTION

All material for the table should be 5/4 select pine. Choose the pieces for the legs. Joint one surface of each piece. Face glue the pieces and clamp them together.

Joint the adjacent edges to develop registration surfaces. Use the planer to produce 2⅛-inch square workpieces. Properly mark the ends for turning. Turn four identical legs (Fig. 16-3). The development and use of a full-sized pattern board is recommended.

Lay out and cut the mortise in the sides of the legs. Each top mortise is ½ × 2 inches. Center and position them ½ inch down from the top. Each bottom mortise is ½ × 1 inch. Center and position them 3¼ inches up from the bottom. Each mortise is ⅞ inch deep.

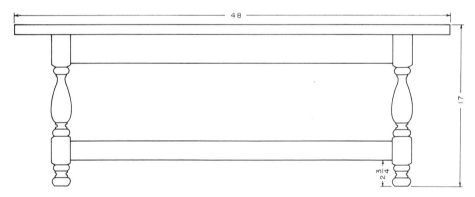

Fig. 16-2. Front view of the Early American coffee table.

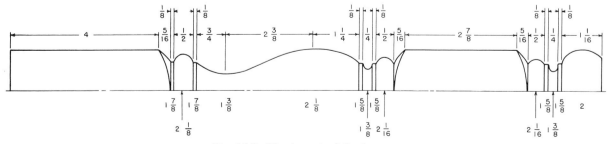

Fig. 16-3. The layout of the leg pattern.

61

BILL OF MATERIAL
Early American Coffee Table—Unit 16
(All dimensions are finished size)

Top	1 pc. 1″ x 20″ x 48″	Pine
Legs	4 pc. 2⅛″ x 2⅛″ x 16″	Pine
Upper		
Rails	2 pc. ⅞″ x 3″ x 15½″	Pine
	2 pc. ⅞″ x 3″ x 37½″	Pine
Lower		
Rails	2 pc. ⅞″ x 2″ x 15½″	Pine
	2 pc. ⅞″ x 2″ x 37½″	Pine
Top		
Fasteners	14 pc.	
Screws	14 pc. Rnd Hd, ¾″, #8	

Cut the material for the rails. Cut tenons on the rail ends with a dado head on the table saw. Set up the blade for the correct depth and position the rail end against the fence. Advance the rail with the miter gauge. Insert each tenon in its corresponding mortise to check for correct fit. Cut a groove in each of the upper rails for the tabletop fasteners. The upper edges of the lower rails should be slightly rounded.

Carry out final sanding of all base pieces. Temporarily assemble the base pieces to check the joint fit and squareness. Glue and clamp the base assembly.

Edge glue the pieces for the top. Plane the top material to the specified thickness and then cut to size. Sand the ends with a belt sander. Boards may be clamped on each side during sanding to assure squareness. Sand down the corners lower than the top surface, to produce a worn look. Center the top on the base assembly and install the screws for the tabletop fasteners. The ends of the top should overhang the base by 4 inches, and the sides should overhang by 1 inch.

FINISHING

Remove the top for final sanding and staining. Apply a dark walnut stain on all surfaces and reinstall the top on the base. Spray on several coats of lacquer sealer. Sand between coats. For the final finish, apply two coats of dull-rubbed finishing lacquer.

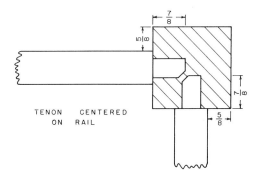

Fig. 16-4. The layout of the top and bottom mortise/tenon joints.

End Tables

The design features and construction of three popular styles of end tables are described in this section. Matching coffee tables and other companion pieces can be constructed from these designs merely by altering the specified dimensions as required.

Unit 17: Early American Step Table

The turned legs and base design of this table match those of the coffee table in Unit 16. The upper section contains two drawers whose fronts are grooved to give the appearance of six smaller drawers. Six porcelain knobs enhance this effect.

Unit 18: Pedestal Table

This versatile accent piece can be used as either an end table or a coffee table. The top may be constructed from solid cherry or it may be made of plywood covered with slate formica. The shape may be either square, as shown here, or hexagonal.

Unit 19: Modern Corner Table

The clean, straight-line design of this table is accented by contrasting materials and open mortise/tenon joints. The framework is solid oak, and the top is a walnut veneered panel.

UNIT 17
Early American Step Table

Fig. 17-1. Early American step table.

The Early American step table in Fig. 17-1 is designed to be a companion to the coffee table in Unit 16. The turned legs and base construction match those of the table in Unit 16. The top section includes two drawers with three porcelain knobs each. The overall height (Fig. 17-2) permits use with a table lamp.

BASE CONSTRUCTION

Select the material for the legs. Joint one surface of each piece. Face glue the pieces and clamp them together. Joint the adjacent edges to develop registration surfaces. Use the planer to produce 2⅛-inch square workpieces. Correctly mark the ends for turning. Turn four identical legs, using the pattern in Fig. 17-3. The development and use of a full-size pattern board is recommended.

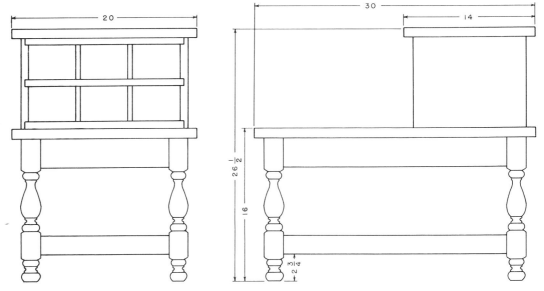

Fig. 17-2. Front and side views of the Early American step table.

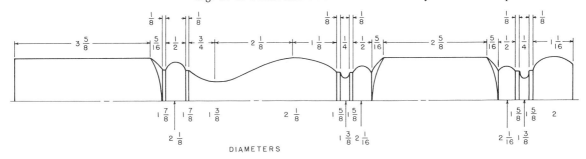

Fig. 17-3. The layout of the leg pattern.

BILL OF MATERIAL
Early American Step Table—Unit 17
(All dimensions are finished size)

Base Structure:

Top			
(Lower)	1 pc.	1″ x 20″ x 30″	Pine
Legs	4 pc.	2⅛″ x 2⅛″ x 15″	Pine
Upper			
Rails	2 pc.	⅞″ x 3″ x 15½″	Pine
	2 pc.	⅞″ x 3″ x 25½″	Pine
Lower			
Rails	2 pc.	⅞″ x 2″ x 15½″	Pine
	2 pc.	⅞″ x 2″ x 25½″	Pine
Top			
Fasteners	14 pc.		
Screws	14 pc.	Round Head, ¾″, #8	

Top Structure:

Top			
(Upper)	1 pc.	1″ x 20″ x 14″	Pine
Case Sides	2 pc.	¾″ x 12″ x 9½″	Pine
Skeleton			
Frames	6 pc.	¾″ x 1½″ x 8¾″	Pine
	6 pc.	¾″ x 1½″ x 17¼″	Pine
Splines	12 pc.	¼″ x ¾″ x 1½″	Fir Plywood
Back	1 pc.	¼″ x 9½″ x 17¼″	Fir Plywood
Screws	16 pc.	Flat Head, 1¼″, #8	

Drawer Parts:

Front	1 pc.	¾″ x 3⅝″ x 16½″	Pine
Back	1 pc.	½″ x 3⅝″ x 16″	Pine
Sides	2 pc.	½″ x 3⅝″ x 11⅜″	Pine
Bottom	1 pc.	¼″ x 11″ x 16″	Fir Plywood
Knobs	6 pc.	Porcelain	

Lay out and cut mortises in the sides of the legs. Each top mortise is ½ x 2 inches. Center and position them ½ inch down from the top. Each bottom mortise is ½ x 1 inch. Center and position them 3¼ inches up from the bottom. The mortises should be cut ⅞ inch deep.

Cut the material for the rails. Cut tenons in the respective rail ends (Fig. 17-4). Use a dado head on the table saw. Set the blade to the required depth, and position the rail end against the fence. Advance the rail with the miter gauge. Insert the tenon in the corresponding mortise to check for correct fit. Cut grooves in the upper rails for the tabletop fasteners. The upper edge of the lower rail should be slightly rounded.

Perform final sanding of all the base pieces. Temporarily assemble the base structure to check joint fit and squareness. Glue the base pieces and clamp them together.

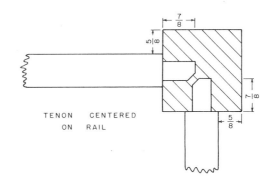

Fig. 17-4. The layout of the mortise/tenon joints.

Fig. 17-6. Hold the stiles upright in a fixture when cutting grooves in their ends.

Select enough material for *both* tops and edge glue it as one piece. Plane the material to the specified thickness and cut it to width. Crosscut the prepared material into two separate pieces, one for the upper top and one for the lower. Sand the ends with a belt sander. During sanding, boards should be clamped on each side to assure squareness. Sand the corners of the tops lower than the top surface, to produce a worn look. Center the lower top on the base assembly and install the screws for the tabletop fasteners. This top should overhang the base by 1 inch on all sides.

TOP SECTION CONSTRUCTION

Select and edge glue the pieces for the case sides. Plane the material to the specified thickness and cut it to size. Cut ⅜-inch-deep dado and rabbet joints in the case sides for insertion of the skeleton frames. Cut ¼ x ⅜-inch rabbets on the back edges of the case sides.

Cut the rails and stiles for the three skeleton frames (Fig. 17-5). Center a ¼ x ⅜-inch groove on one edge of each rail. Cut an identical groove on both ends of the stiles. Hold the pieces upright in a fixture while cutting the end grooves (Fig. 17-6). Glue and assemble the skeleton frame pieces with splines.

Drill and countersink screw holes in the top skeleton frame for

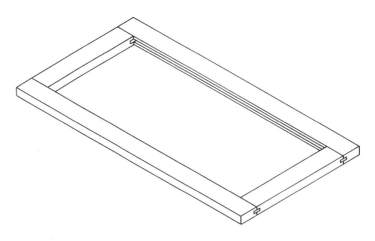

Fig. 17-5. Construction of the skeleton frames.

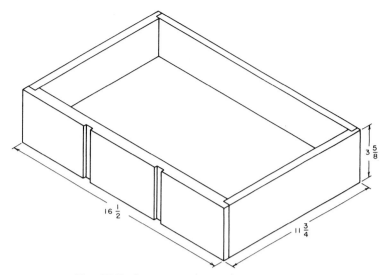

Fig. 17-7. Construction of the drawers.

attachment of the top. Trial fit the case pieces to check the joint fit and squareness. Glue and assemble the case pieces, then clamp with bar clamps. Center the top surface on the case and attach it with screws. The top should overhang the case by 1 inch on all sides. Correctly position the top section on the base and attach it with screws. Space the top section 1 inch from the sides and back of the base. Cut the case back from ¼-inch plywood.

DRAWER CONSTRUCTION

Cut the pieces for the drawers (Fig. 17-7). Cut a groove for the bottom ¼ inch up from the edge of all pieces. Cut a ½-inch rabbet on the ends of the front. Cut the rabbets ⅜ inch deep. Cut a ½-inch rabbet on one end of each side. Cut these rabbets ¼ inch deep. Simulate three small drawers by cutting two evenly spaced dado grooves across each drawer front. Cut the grooves ¼ x ½ inch with a router. Cut and fit the bottom piece. Glue and assemble the drawers with finish nails.

FINISHING

Disassemble the structural pieces and perform final sanding and staining. After sanding, apply dark walnut stain to all visible areas. Attach the top with screws and tabletop fasteners. Attach the back with brads, then spray on several coats of lacquer sealer. Sand between the sealer coats. For a final finish, apply two coats of dull-rubbed finish lacquer. Install the procelain knobs on the drawer fronts.

UNIT 18
Pedestal Table

*Fig. 18-*1. Pedestal table which can be used either as a coffee or end table.

The pedestal table in Fig. 18-1 is designed to serve as an accent piece. These table types often are used in pairs. The size (Fig. 18-2) permits use as either a coffee table or an end table. The top may be constructed from solid cherry or it may be plywood covered with slate formica. The shape may be square or hexagonal.

CONSTRUCTION

Select the material for the pedestal as specified in the *Bill of Material*. Cut the pieces to rough size then joint the surfaces to be glued. Face glue and clamp together the pieces.

Joint the adjacent edges to develop registration surfaces. Use the planer to produce a 5⅝-inch square workpiece. Square the ends and correctly mark them for turning. Cut off the corners at a 45-degree angle. Turn the workpiece according to the plan provided in Fig. 18-3. Development of a full-size pattern board is recommended.

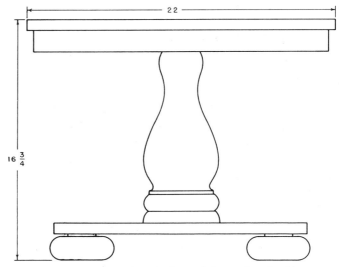

Fig. 18-2. Dimensioned view of the pedestal table.

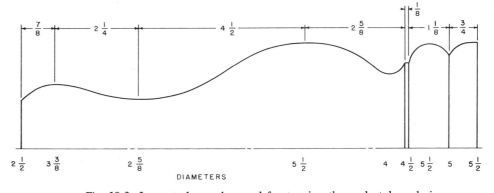

Fig. 18-3. Layout plan to be used for turning the pedestal workpiece.

BILL OF MATERIAL
Pedestal Table—Unit 18
(All dimensions are finished size)

Pedestal	1 pc.	5⅝" x 5⅝" x 12¼"	Cherry
Base	1 pc.	¾" x 18" x 18"	Cherry
Foot	4 pc.	1¾" x 4½" x 4½"	Cherry
Top Apron	4 pc.	¾" x 1½" x 21"	Cherry
Top Support	1 pc.	1" x 4½" x 19½"	Poplar
Top Surface	1 pc.	¾" x 22" x 22"	Marble
Splines	4 pc.	¼" x ¾" x 1½" ·	Fir Plywood
Dowel Pins	8 pc.	⅜" x 1½"	Birch
Screws	6 pc.	Flat Head, 1¾", #10	

Fig. 18-4. A view of the partially completed pedestal table which shows the construction of the top structure.

Select the material for the top apron. Joint and plane it to the specified thickness, then rip it to width. Cut it to the specified length, with a 45-degree angle on the ends.

Cut the grooves for the splines. Use the edge miter and a ¼-inch dado head. Tilt the dado head to 45 degrees. Place the end to cut against the fence. Correctly position the groove. Set the depth of cut to ⅜ inch. Advance the workpiece with the miter gauge. Be sure to back up all pieces with an auxiliary board.

Select the material for the top support. Joint and plane it to the specified thickness. Cut it to the required width and length, then drill holes in the ends for the ⅜ inch dowels. Position the support in the top frame ¼ inch up from the bottom edges and centered (Fig. 18-4). Position the matching holes with dowel centers. Perform a trial assembly, then glue the pieces, insert the splines, and clamp together the assembly.

Edge glue the pieces for the base. Plane the workpiece to the required thickness and then cut it to size. Prepare to enlarge the base pattern in Fig. 18-5 to finished size. Rule 1-inch squares on a heavy piece of paper. Letter the vertical lines in Fig. 18-5, and number the horizontal lines. Place corresponding letters and numbers on the full-size pattern grid. Transfer points on the pattern in Fig. 18-5 to the full-size pattern grid. When it is completed, lay the full-size pattern on the base workpiece and

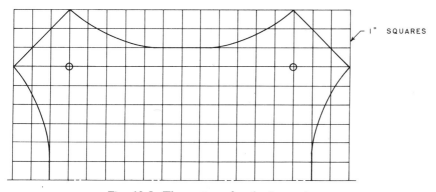

1" SQUARES

Fig. 18-5. The pattern for the base piece.

End Tables

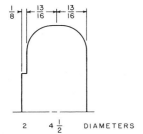

Fig. 18-6. The pattern for the feet.

trace around it. Cut around the layout lines with the band saw and then sand. Drill ⅜-inch holes for attachment of the feet. Shape all edges with a ⅜ rounding over bit in the router.

Select the material for the feet. Correctly prepare the workpiece for faceplate turning. Turn according to the plan provided in Fig. 18-6. Drill ⅜-inch holes for the dowels.

FINISHING

Carry out the final sanding of all parts. Attach the top assembly and base to the pedestal with screws. Glue the feet, insert the dowels, and clamp the feet to the base.

Apply Early American brown stain. Spray on several coats of lacquer sealer. Sand between the sealer coats. For a final finish, apply two coats of dull-gloss finishing lacquer.

UNIT 19
Modern Corner Table

Fig. 19-1. Modern-style corner table.

The modern styling of the corner table in Fig. 19-1 is established by the clean, straight-line design. Contrasting materials add an interesting ingredient to the simple lines. The framework is oak, and the top is a walnut veneered panel. Open mortise/tenon joints also accent the design (Figs. 19-2 and 19-3).

CONSTRUCTION

Cut the oak structural pieces to rough size. Joint the adjacent edges to develop registration surfaces. Use the planer to assure uniform thickness of all structural pieces. Cut the legs and cross members to the finished lengths specified in the *Bill of Material.*

Cut the mortises in the pieces for the leg structure. The mortises are cut on the upright pieces and the tenons on the cross member (Fig. 19-4). Cut the open mortises with a tenon attachment on the table saw (Fig. 19-5). A 10-inch saw blade will provide the required depth of cut.

Fig. 19-2. Open mortise/tenon joints are used to mate the main structural members.

Make initial cuts on each side of the mortise. Clean out the mortise with additional cuts. Reset the tenon attachment and make the cheek cuts on the tenon. Complete the shoulder cut with the piece lying flat on the saw. Carefully fit the tenon to the mortise. Backup boards should be used during all cuts, to avoid chipping.

Filing will be needed to eliminate saw marks in the joints. An easy slip fit is desired. Extremely tight joints will not allow enough

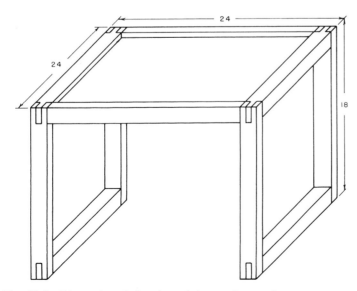

Fig. 19-3. Dimensioned drawing of the modern-style corner table.

BILL OF MATERIAL
Modern Corner Table—Unit 19
(All dimensions are finished size)

Legs	4 pc. 1¾″ x 1¾″ x 18″	Oak
Cross Members	4 pc. 1¾″ x 1¾″ x 24″	Oak
Cross Members	2 pc. 1¾″ x 1¾″ x 20½″	Oak
Dowels	4 pc. ⅝″ x 2½″	Birch
Top	1 pc. ½″ x 21″ x 21″	Fir Plywood
	2 pc. 21″ x 21″	Walnut Veneer
Cleats	2 pc. ¾″ x ¾″ x 20¼″	Oak
	2 pc. ¾″ x ¾″ x 18½″	Oak
Screws	8 pc. Flat Head, 1″, #8	
	12 pc. Flat Head, 1½″ #8	

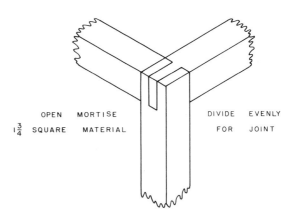

OPEN MORTISE
1¾ SQUARE MATERIAL

DIVIDE EVENLY
FOR JOINT

Fig. 19-4. The layout of the open mortise/tenon joints.

space for the glue. Apply plastic resin glue to the joints and secure them with bar clamps during drying. Apply face pressure to each joint with parallel clamps. These procedures assure a strong, neat joint.

Attach the cross members to the leg structure with dowels. Place one dowel in each joint. Use dowel centers to correctly position the matching dowel holes. Surrations should be filed around the dowel, and the ends should be beveled. These procedures ensure better glue distribution and, therefore, greater holding power. Clamp the joints without glue, to check for correct fit and squareness. Make any necessary alterations to the joints *before* gluing them.

VENEERING

Prepare to fabricate the veneered walnut top panel. Use ½-inch plywood. Veneer both the face and the back surface, to assure a stable workpiece. Make the top oversize for trimming later.

Select the veneer for the face and back surfaces. Joint the veneer edges on the jointer. Clamp the veneer between plywood pieces during this operation (Fig. 19-6). Tape the veneer splices and splits

Fig. 19-5. A tenon attachment for cutting open mortise/tenon joints on the table saw.

Fig. 19-6. Clamp the veneer between plywood pieces when jointing it.

with brown paper tape. Place the tape on the outside surface, for easy removal later. Be sure to use brown paper tape; *do not use masking tape.* (Pressure would force the masking tape into the wood pores.) Use plastic resin glue for attaching the veneer to the plywood surfaces. If a means of applying pressure is not available, use contact cement.

The amounts of glue and water to be mixed are dependent on the number of square feet to be covered. In this case, there are four 3.1-square-foot surfaces, or a total of 12.4 square feet. Use 12.5 grams of glue per square foot and 7.5 grams of water. The mixture, therefore, should consist of 155 grams of glue and 93 grams of water.

Add the water to the glue a small amount at a time. Brush on enough of the mixture to make the surfaces appear well wetted. Press the veneer to the plywood, and allow sufficient drying time. After drying is complete, trim the veneered top to fit into the table frame. Carefully scrape off the tape and sand the top surface. Inset the top panel ½ inch below the upper frame surface. Attach the top to the table frame with cleats.

FINISHING

Perform final sanding of all surfaces. Sand off all sharp corners. Finish the surfaces with Danish oil.

COMPANION TABLE DIMENSIONS

Other sizes of this table may be constructed to serve as companion pieces. A suggested coffee table size is 24 x 48 inches, with a height of 15 or 16 inches. The recommended dimensions for a matching rectangular end table are 20 x 24 inches, with a height of 20 or 22 inches.

SECTION VIII

Student Planning

The wood furniture projects in this section give the student an opportunity to determine material requirements, plan specific construction procedures and create design variations. The special design features of each project are described, and general guidelines are given for construction. However, the development of a Bill of Material and the planning of specific procedures are left to the student. To direct the student's creative thinking, variations of sizes, trims, finishes and other design possibilities are suggested.

Unit 20: Enclosures

Unit 21: Open Tool Box

Unit 22: Boxes

Unit 23: Display Cabinets

Unit 24: Chests

Unit 25: Collection Boxes

Fig. 20-1. An enclosure designed to house a 6-inch speaker.

UNIT 20
Enclosure

The enclosure shown in Figs. 20-1 and 20-2 is designed to house a 6-inch speaker. Use ¾-inch-thick material and strengthen all joints with cleats. The inside should be insulated with fiber glass or foam. This will make the enclosure distortion-free.

CONSTRUCTION

Material for the sides, top and bottom is machined with a 15-degree bevel on the front edge. The bevel slants inward to produce a picture frame effect. The back edge has a rabbet for the ¼-inch-thick back panel. Variations of this design include reversal of the bevel or routing of the inner edges.

Tilt the table saw blade to cut the miter joints. Cut the joints with the good side up, to avoid chipping. Cut one end of all pieces. Use a stop block when cutting the pieces to length. Attach it to the auxiliary board of the miter gauge. This will assure that the pieces are identical.

Cut all cleats from ¾-inch-square material and pre-drill them. Cut the back panel from ¼-inch plywood. Cut the front panel from ½-inch plywood. Make the front panel ⅛ inch less than the opening size.

ASSEMBLY

Glue and screw the cleats to the larger sides. Set the cleats for the front panel back ¾ inch from the decorative edge (Fig. 20-2). Position the cleats to strengthen the joints at the edge of the miter. Cleats for the front panel also are placed on the top and bottom

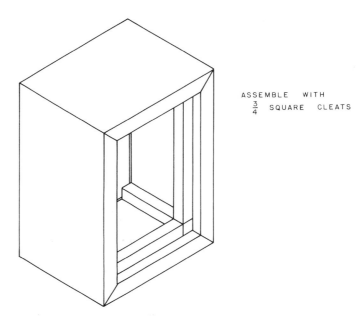

ASSEMBLE WITH
¾ SQUARE CLEATS

Fig. 20-2. Construction of the speaker enclosure.

pieces. Carry out final assembly with picture frame clamps. Glue the miters and corner cleats, and install screws.

FINISHING

Apply the desired types of stain and finish material. Mount the speaker and attach the grill cloth. Wrap the grill cloth around the edge of the panel and staple it to the back. Install the wiring and insulation, then attach the back with screws.

The spice rack in Fig. 20-3 is another variation of an enclosure which uses miter joints and a rabbeted back. Cleats usually are not used if the inside is exposed and is to be finished. Instead, a series of *feathers* are used to strengthen the miter joint. Cut the feathers after gluing the cabinet. An exposed or stopped spline also can be used.

Fig. 20-3. Spice rack variation of the basic enclosure. Feathers are used in the miter joints in place of the cleats.

Fig. 21-1. An open tool box designed for small hand tools.

UNIT 21
Open Tool Box

The open tool box in Figs. 21-1 and 21-2 is made for small hand tools. The design of this project can be altered to suit many purposes. The variations include a machinist's tool box, a home tool tote, a model airplane box, and a battery box. Additions to the basic design include partitions, tool holders, lids and drawers.

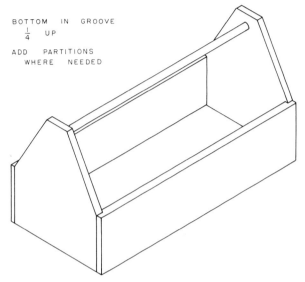

```
BOTTOM  IN  GROOVE
   1
   ─  UP
   4

ADD   PARTITIONS
   WHERE   NEEDED
```

Fig. 21-2. Rabbet joints in the ends of the sides are used to mate the main structural members.

CONSTRUCTION

A general-purpose hardwood is normally used for such boxes. The wide ends require edge-to-edge gluing. Most boxes are made with ¾- or ⅝-inch-thick material. The bottom typically is ½-inch fir plywood.

Square all pieces before cutting the joints. Cut a ½-inch groove for the plywood bottom on all pieces. Cut the grooves ¼ inch up from the bottom edge. Cut rabbet joints on the ends of the sides. Drill holes for the handle halfway through the end pieces. Bandsaw and sand the slant on the ends.

ASSEMBLY AND FINISHING

Assemble the pieces with glue and clamp them. The handle may be left loose enough to turn. If partitions are used, position and anchor them with finish nails. Sand the surfaces and apply polyurethane varnish.

78

UNIT 22
Box

The basic box structure of the tool chest in Fig. 22-1 is joined exclusively with rabbet joints. The construction is simple and easily understood. The tool chest is one of many possible variations of the basic box. Larger chests are made entirely of plywood. Fine hardwoods are used for smaller variations such as jewel chests and trinket boxes.

CONSTRUCTION

The material used for the tool chest is poplar. The material thickness is ⅝ inch, to limit the weight. The partitions are made from ½-inch poplar (Fig. 22-2). The bottom is made from ½-inch fir plywood.

Square all stock. Cut a ½-inch rabbet on the bottom edge of all pieces. Cut a ⅝ rabbet on the ends of the front and back pieces. Glue and assemble the sides and bottom, then clamp them in place.

Edge glue the top piece and plane it to ⅝-inch thickness. Cut the top to exactly fit the box. Cut a ⅝-inch rabbet on all edges of the top. The top should easily drop into place over the side pieces. Glue and clamp the top in place.

Fig. 22-1. Box-type tool chest constructed of poplar pieces mated with rabbet joints.

Fig. 22-2. The number and placement of tool chest compartments are up to the student.

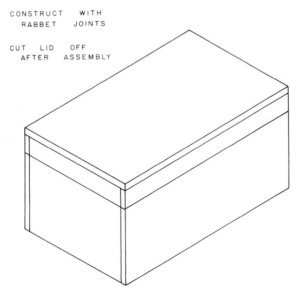

CONSTRUCT WITH
RABBET JOINTS

CUT LID OFF
AFTER ASSEMBLY

Fig. 22-3. The top section is separated from the bottom part by ripping on the table saw after the glued box assembly has dried.

79

Sand all corners square. Set up the table saw for ripping. Cut off the top section, one side at a time. Sand the edges to eliminate saw marks.

FINAL ASSEMBLY AND FINISHING

Machine and fit the desired partitions (Fig. 22-3). After positioning, anchor them with finish nails. Perform final sanding of the surfaces, and sand off all sharp corners. Apply a polyurethane varnish finish. Install the desired hardware when the finish has dried.

BACKGAMMON CASE

The backgammon case in Fig. 22-4 is a variation of the rabbet-joined box. The structural material is ½-inch-thick mahogany. The panels are ¼-inch-thick mahogany plywood. The playing area (Fig. 22-5) is veneer pieces glued in place. (This case design also can be modified to serve as a drawing case or a case for oil paints and brushes.)

The case in Figs. 22-4 and 22-5 provides a 12 x 16-inch inside dimension. The case height is 3 inches overall. Triangles for the play area are 2 inches wide by 6 inches high. The playing pieces are 1-inch dowel.

Construct the case with rabbet joints at the corners. Place the panels in grooves cut in the sides. Cut the grooves ¼ inch in from the edge of all side pieces. Glue and clamp the assembly. Sand all corners square.

After the glued assembly dries, cut the case into two halves. Rip it on the table saw, one side at a time. Sand the edges to eliminate saw marks. Cut and apply the veneer triangles, and finish the case with several coats of polyurethane varnish. Attach the desired hardware when the finish has dried.

Fig. 22-4. The structural pieces of this box-type backgammon case are mated with rabbet joints.

Fig. 22-5. The playing surface of the backgammon case is made from glued-in-place veneer pieces.

UNIT 23
Display Cabinet

The small cabinet in Figs. 23-1 and 23-2 is designed especially for display storage of mugs. Construction is kept simple through the use of butt and rabbet joints. The cabinet is decorated with a routed top and bottom.

CONSTRUCTION

Material for the sides is ⅜-inch mahogany. The pieces to be routed are ½ inch thick. The back is ⅛-inch hardboard.

Cut the sides and center partitions. Cut an edge lap to lock together the partitions. Cut a ⅛-inch rabbet on the back edge of the sides.

Fig. 23-1. Small display/storage cabinet for mugs.

Fig. 23-3. A three-shelf display/storage cabinet for a larger mug collection.

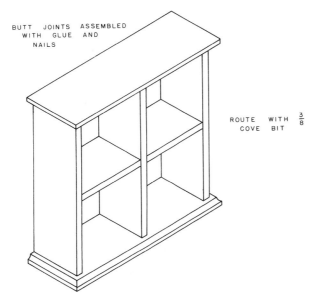

BUTT JOINTS ASSEMBLED WITH GLUE AND NAILS

ROUTE WITH $\frac{3}{8}$ COVE BIT

Fig. 23-2. Construction of the small display/storage cabinet.

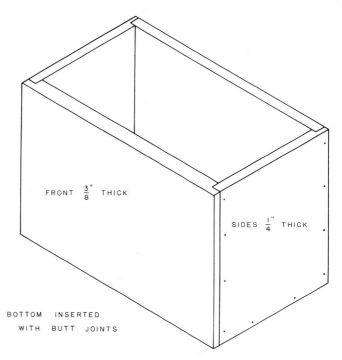

FRONT $\frac{3}{8}$" THICK

SIDES $\frac{1}{4}$" THICK

BOTTOM INSERTED
WITH BUTT JOINTS

Fig. 23-4. Construction of the drawers for the three-shelf display/storage cabinet.

Measure and cut the top and bottom pieces to provide a ⅝-inch overhang. Shape the front and the edges with a ⅜ cove bit. Cut a *blind rabbet* in the back edges with a straight bit in the router/shaper table.

Assemble the cabinet with glue and finish nails. Attach the back with brads. Finish with Danish oil.

THREE-SHELF VARIATION

The three-shelf cabinet in Fig. 23-3 is designed to display a larger mug collection. Small drawers (Fig. 23-4) are added to the basic cabinet design.

The material is pine with a dark Early American finish. The back is made from ¼-inch pine boards beveled to simulate paneling. All parts are sanded unevenly to produce a worn look.

UNIT 24
Chest

The chests described in this unit use splined miter joints to join the structural pieces. The jewel chest in Figs. 24-1 and 24-2 is one of many design variations. Larger chests may include a drawer in the lower area. Other popular additions include decorative surface molding, ornate leg treatment and various styles of hardware.

CONSTRUCTION

The material is ½-inch-thick walnut. The top panel is hardboard with walnut veneer surfaces. The bottom is ¼-inch hardboard.

Machine the material to the required thicknesses and widths. Tilt the table saw to cut the miter joints. Cut miters in one end of all structural pieces. Use a stop block when cutting the sides to length.

Fig. 24-1. Jewel chest constructed with splined miter joints.

Fig. 24-3. The number and positioning of partitions in the jewel chest are up to the student.

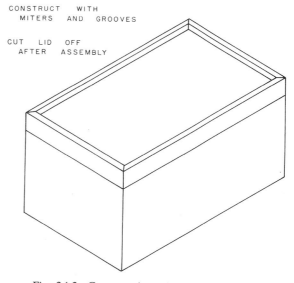

CONSTRUCT WITH
MITERS AND GROOVES

CUT LID OFF
AFTER ASSEMBLY

Fig. 24-2. Construction of the jewel chest.

83

Fig. 24-4. A smaller chest with blind-splined miter joints, and molding around the top panel.

Attach the block to the auxiliary board of the miter gauge. This will assure that the sides are identical.

Use a dado head to cut grooves for the top and bottom panels in the side pieces. Be sure the width of the top grooves fits the veneered panel. Position the bottom grooves to allow for cutting out the legs.

Cut the grooves for the spline in the edge miter with a ¼-inch dado head. Tilt the dado head to 45 degrees. Place the end being cut against the fence. Correctly position the groove and set the blade depth. Advance the workpiece with the miter gauge. Cut out the decorative feet and sand the surfaces.

ASSEMBLY AND FINISHING

Assemble the chest with ¼-inch plywood splines. Leave the splines short enough to permit plugging on the top. Glue and clamp the assembly with picture frame clamps.

Set up the table saw for ripping, then cut off the top section, one side at a time. Sand the edges to eliminate saw marks.

Machine and fit the desired partitions (Fig. 24-3). Cut appropriate joints where needed. Position the partitions and glue them in place. Apply a Danish oil finish and install the hardware.

A SMALLER CHEST

The smaller chest in Fig. 24-4 is a variation of the basic chest construction. A blind spline is used in the miter joints. Molding is placed around the top panel.

To produce the molding, rout the edge of a wide board. Rip off the molding piece from the board with the table saw. Position the good piece on the outside of the blade and reset the fence for each cut.

UNIT 25
Collection Box

Fig. 25-1. A collection box for displaying model trains.

The collection boxes in this unit are designed to display particular types of items. The box in Fig. 25-1 is completely closed by a glass front. A removable frame over the glass provides easy access to the displayed items.

CONSTRUCTION

The type of material used should compliment the displayed items. The sides are planed to ⅜-inch thickness. All partitions are ¼-inch thick. The back material is ⅛-inch hardboard.

Cut and assemble the top, bottom and side pieces, with rabbet joints at the corners (Fig. 25-2). Place the back in a ⅛-inch rabbet joint. Cut and fit the partitions in the desired positions. Apply glue to the partitions, then anchor them with finish nails. Cut the glass to fit.

The frame for the glass is made from contrasting material. Machine it into ¼ x ½-inch strips (Fig. 25-3). Cut the pieces to fit

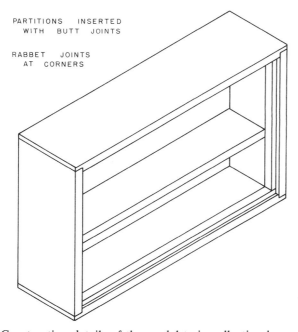

PARTITIONS INSERTED
WITH BUTT JOINTS

RABBET JOINTS
AT CORNERS

Fig. 25-2. Construction details of the model train collection box.

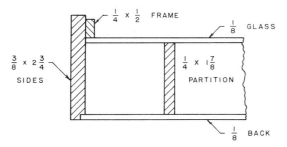

$\frac{1}{4}$ x $\frac{1}{2}$ FRAME

$\frac{1}{8}$ GLASS

$\frac{3}{8}$ x 2$\frac{3}{4}$
SIDES

$\frac{1}{4}$ x 1$\frac{7}{8}$
PARTITION

$\frac{1}{8}$ BACK

Fig. 25-3. Cross-sectional top view of the model train collection box.

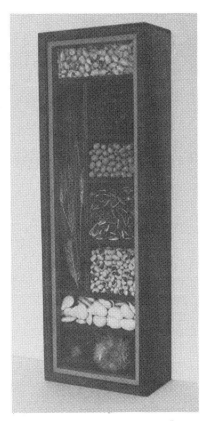

Fig. 25-4. An ecology box for displaying seeds and flowers.

Fig. 25-5. A collection box for displaying cones.

easily inside the box. Use an end lap for stronger corner joints. Place one screw in each side piece to hold the frame in place.

ECOLOGY BOX

The ecology box in Fig. 25-4 is a variation of the previously described construction. The partitions are positioned to provide ample space for each type of displayed item. The frame for the glass front can be painted a color which compliments the collection. All finishing should be completed before filling the box with seeds and flowers.

COLLECTION BOX

The collection box for cones in Fig. 25-5 is another variation. Spaces are provided for various cones. The material used is very knotty spruce. It is left natural, without a finish. The glass-closed box eliminates a dust problem.

Glossary of Wood Furniture Terms

Apron. Protruding *horizontal* trim positioned between the case and the feet of a wood furniture structure.

Box Joint (or finger joint). A type of joint which secures two perpendicularly positioned boards by means of alternate, tightly fitting, finger-like protrusions and matching recesses cut in the ends of the boards.

Butt Joint. A type of joint in which the matching square edges of two boards are placed against each other and secured by metal fasteners or other means.

Cleat. A length of predrilled, ¾-inch-square wood or other material which is positioned and secured along the inside corner of a joint to strengthen it.

Composition Material. A type of material formed by mixing two or more types of ingredients and bonding them together by pressure, glue and/or other means. Woods and plastics are two common types of ingredients used in composition material.

Compound Miter Joint. A cut made across a board at angles to both the width and the thickness of the board. Compound miter joints are made by setting the table-saw miter gauge at an angle and tilting the saw blade.

Cove Cut. A rounded (or concave) groove cut in the surface and *along* the grain of a board.

Crosscut (with a saw). A cut made *across* the grain and perpendicular to the registration surface of a board.

Dado Head. A table saw accessory which is used to cut a rectangular groove in a board. (Also see *Dado Joint.*)

Dado Joint. The mating of two perpendicularly positioned boards by means of a rectangular groove cut across the grain and in from the end of one board, into which groove is fitted the end of the other board (or a matching protrusion cut in the end of the other board).

Dowel. A round, wooden connecting pin which fits into corresponding holes drilled into the mated edges of two boards which are to be joined. (Also see *Dowel Joint.*)

Dowel Joint. A joint which is strengthened by round, wooden pins glued in corresponding holes drilled in the mated edges of two joined boards. (Also see *Dowel.*)

Edge Banding. Thin strips of material which are used to cover the edges of cabinet tops.

87

Edge-To-Edge Gluing. The mating of boards by gluing their corresponding edges and then pressing together the glued edges to form a single, wider surface.

Facing. Wooden strips ¼ to ¾ inch thick which are used to cover the exposed edges of plywood or the front surfaces of cabinets.

Feather. A thin, wooden piece which is placed in matching grooves cut *across* and *perpendicular* to the joint surface, to strengthen the joint.

Free Form. A form, or shape, created by hand *without* the aid of tools which produce a specific, predetermined design.

Jointing. The process of smoothing and truing the edge of a board by running it across the cutting blades of a jointer.

Keyed Tenon. A protrusion (tenon) on the end of a board which extends through and beyond a matching hole (mortise) in another board a sufficient amount to permit the insertion of a locking crosspiece (key) in the protrusion. (Also see *Mortise/Tenon Joint* and *Tenon.*)

Lap Joint. A flush, face-to-face joint made by cutting away opposite halves of the ends or edges of two boards and then overlapping the resultant protrusions and recesses.

Miter. A cut made at an angle to either the width or the thickness of a board. (Also see *Miter Joint.*)

Miter Joint. A joint formed by making matching angular cuts in two pieces and fitting them together. The angle of miter cuts typically is 45 degrees from a line across the width or thickness of the mated boards, although other angles also are used. (Also see *Miter.*)

Mortise. A hole cut in a board into which is inserted a matching protrusion (tenon) cut in the end of another board. (Also see *Mortise/Tenon Joint, Tenon* and *Through Mortise.*)

Mortise/Tenon Joint. An exceptionally strong joint formed by cutting a hole (mortise) in one board and inserting into it a matching protrusion (tenon) cut in the end of another board. Mortise/tenon joints typically are used to join the legs and rail of a table or bench. (Also see *Mortise* and *Tenon.*)

Ogee. A router bit which produces an S-shaped curve on the outer surface of trim pieces.

Rabbet. An L-shaped (or two-sided) cut made in the edge or end of a board. (Also see *Rabbet Joint.*)

Rabbet Joint. A joint formed by making an L-shaped (or two-sided) cut in the edge or end of one board and inserting into it the square edge or end of another board. A typical use of rabbet joints is in the corners of a box. (Also see *Rabbet.*)

Rail. The horizontal supporting member of a frame or other structure. The rails of a frame typically are attached to and separated by the panels and stiles (vertical members) of the frame. (Also see *Stile.*)

Ratchet Mechanism. A member into whose edge is cut tooth-like notches which catch and prevent slippage of a lever-like member. Ratchet mechanisms typically are used in wood furniture to prop up a table top or other surface at various preselected angles.

Rip (with a saw). A cut made *with* the grain and parallel to the registration edge of a board. (Also see *Crosscut.*)

Sapwood. That portion of wood which is formed between the outer layers and the heartwood of a tree, and which usually is softer and has a lighter coloration than is typical of the heartwood of that particular species.

Spline. A thin wooden strip placed in a matching groove cut parallel to the surface of a joint, to strengthen the joint.

Splined Miter Joint. A joint formed by making matching angular cuts in the two boards to be joined, and then strengthening the joint by inserting a thin wooden strip (spline) into grooves cut in the mated surfaces of the joint. (Also see *Spline* and *Miter Joint.*)

Stile. One of the *vertical* members of a frame, into which are fitted the rails (horizontal members). (Also see *Rails.*)

Stop Dado. A rectangular groove which is cut *across* the grain of a board from one edge to a point short of the other edge. (Also see *Dado Joint* and *Dado Head.*)

Tenon. A rectangular protrusion cut in the end of one board for insertion into a matching hole (mortise) cut in another board. (Also see *Mortise, Mortise/Tenon Joint* and *Through Mortise.*)

Through Mortise. A rectangular hole cut *completely through* the thickness of a board, into which is inserted a protrusion (tenon) cut in the end of another board. Because the protrusion extends completely through the hole (through mortise), its end is visible. (Also see *Mortise, Mortise/Tenon Joint* and *Tenon.*)

Trim. Material used for decorating the exposed surfaces and/or edges of a cabinet or other furniture structure. Trim may be left square or it may be shaped with a router.

Veneer. A thin layer of wood which typically is used to cover less attractive and/or less durable wood. Veneer ranges from $1/100$ to $1/4$ inch thick and typically is attached by gluing.

Veneered Plywood. Plywood constructed of layers of veneer whose grains are positioned at right angles to each other, with one or both exposed sides covered with select cabinet veneer. (Also see *Veneer.*)

Metric Equivalents of Fractional Inches

(1 inch = 25.4 millimeters)

Fractional Inches	*Millimeters*
$^1/_{16}$	1.587
$^1/_8$	3.175
$^3/_{16}$	4.762
$^1/_4$	6.350
$^5/_{16}$	7.937
$^3/_8$	9.525
$^7/_{16}$	11.112
$^1/_2$	12.700
$^9/_{16}$	14.283
$^5/_8$	15.875
$^{11}/_{16}$	17.462
$^3/_4$	19.050
$^{13}/_{16}$	20.637
$^7/_8$	22.225
$^{15}/_{16}$	23.812

Inch-Metric/Metric-Inch Conversion Factors

To convert:	*multiply by:*
Inches to millimeters	25.4
Inches to centimeters	2.54
Inches to meters	0.0254
Millimeters to inches	0.03937
Centimeters to inches	0.3937
Meters to inches	39.37
Sq. inches to sq. centimeters	6.4516
Sq. centimeters to sq. inches	0.155